When the Wind is Against You

Encouragement for When Life Pushes Back

Stephen D. McConnell

ISBN 13: 9781492175162
ISBN: 1492175161
Library of Congress Control Number: 2013915536
CreateSpace Independent Publishing Platform
North Charleston, South Carolina

To the communities of faith with whom I've served. The teaching has been yours, the learning has been mine.

CONTENTS

$\mathscr{P}$ R E F A C E

"BE OF GOOD cheer." That was the farewell my father used for as long as I remember. Whenever he had a good-bye to say it was always, "Be of good cheer." For a long time I thought of it as a nice positive parting and didn't think to consider its origin. For as much as I guessed, it originated with him. It wasn't until I was a little older that I stumbled upon the words in a Sunday School lesson. It turns out that they are the words of Jesus spoken to his disciples on the night of his betrayal and trial. The context was surprising along with the fact that they are a part of a larger exhortation. The full utterance of Christ is this: "In this world *you will have trouble*, but **be of good cheer**, for I have overcome the world." (John 16:33) Now all of a sudden this fond farewell became something different for me. It was a call to something greater. It was an appeal to hope in the face of difficulty. You will have tough times, Christ was saying, life will push back, the world will not always agree with you, but take heart for God in Christ helps us to endure.

I thought of this when visiting the grave of C.S. Lewis in Headington Quarry outside of Oxford. He is buried in the small churchyard of Holy Trinity Church where he and his brother Warnie worshipped most Sunday mornings. The grave is covered by a simple rectangular marble slab upon which Warnie had inscribed the words: "Men must endure their going hence." It's a line from Shakespeare's *King Lear* and they were the words on the page of their mother's Shakespeare calendar the day she died. They were just boys when she died and it was an event that changed them forever. Yet they kept those words between them, likely as an encouragement to each other, as if to say – the world brings its difficulty but we endure it with courage, for Christ has ultimately won the battle.

Serving as a pastor I am given the opportunity to come alongside of people at the most important moments of their lives. Some are times of joy: birth, baptism, marriage, anniversaries, graduations. Others are times of hurt and crisis: illness, divorce, dying and grief. I have seen good things happen to bad people and bad things happen to good people. The world is rather indiscriminate in what it does to its inhabitants, and people of faith are not immune to trouble. In the face of pain I seldom, if ever, have the answer to the questions of why. The best I have to offer is the hope of believing that the One who entered the world in Christ and defeated the powers of darkness, promises to walk with us in the pain. "In this world you will have trouble, but take courage, for he is here and he has overcome the powers of the world."

From the moment our mothers delivered us from the womb life has pushed back. We learned early that we were not the center of the universe. Events often conspire to make us doubt ourselves and our place in the world. Dreams of youth can dissipate and we can despair over what has not happened for us. Nevertheless, we try to endure and in our attempt to do so we appeal to something higher and greater to get us through.

No words outside of scripture have resonated for me more than those of Victor Frankl, survivor of Auschwitz, when reflecting in his seminal *Man's Search for Meaning* on the epiphany that got him through the worst of all human sufferings, he wrote: "What was really needed was a fundamental change in our attitude toward life. We had to learn ourselves and, furthermore, we had to teach the despairing men, that *it did not really matter what we expected from life, but rather what life expected from us.*" Our endurance, our pressing on, gives testimony that life is more than a string of accidents. Life expects something from us! There is purpose and for the person of faith the purpose is found in the One who creates, loves, redeems and overcomes the world.

I hope these chapters prove an encouragement to you as you face into a life that often pushes back. If in them you find a little comfort, a reason to hope and a challenge to change then glory be to God. Above all it is my hope that you discover again that you are an extraordinary creation of God whose purpose is to overcome with Christ and encourage others to do the same.

Be of good cheer.

$\mathcal{A}$ $\mathcal{L}$AUGHING $\mathcal{M}$ATTER

Genesis 18:1–15

THE STORY IS told of a young Ivy League graduate interviewing for his first job at a firm in New York City, and as the interview came to a close the human resources person conducting the interview asked the young graduate, "Now, what starting salary were you looking for?"

And the young graduate replied, "Oh, somewhere in the neighborhood of $250,000 a year, depending on the benefits package."

The interviewer said, "Well, what would you say to a package of six weeks' vacation, fourteen paid holidays, full medical and dental, company matching retirement fund up to 50 percent of salary, and a company car leased every two years—whatever you want . . . Mercedes, BMW, Volvo, you name it."

The young graduate sat straight up in his chair and said, "Wow! Are you kidding?"

And the interviewer replied, "Yeah, but you started it."

I have a question for you: How much are you worth? Are you worth $250,000? Are you worth double that? Are you worth half that? And where would you go to find out? I find myself in conversations every once in a while where we get to talking about some person who is making a gazillion dollars doing something—professional sports, business, stock market—and the comment that invariably comes out of somebody's mouth is, "Man, nobody is worth that kind of money." Is that true? Do we really believe that? If a child needs a life-saving operation that is going to cost a gazillion dollars, would we say the same thing? "Nobody is worth that kind of money?"

How much are you worth?

It's a shame, isn't it, that too often that question gets answered only in terms of dollars and cents. It is a shame that the question only gets answered when it is contract-negotiating time or salary-increase time. *What am I worth?* This will be determined by my boss, the company earnings, and the increase in the cost of living. Some make out real well in those categories and some don't. It's a shame, isn't it, that our question of worth gets answered so often in terms of compensatory bottom line?

Sometimes it gets answered in hair coloring when the L'oréal woman comes on the TV and says, "But I'm worth it." A lot of times it gets determined inside the walls of our homes. When we're growing up we look to our parents to give us some indication of our worth. And again, some make out better in this situation than others. Some parents know how to reinforce a child's worth and others don't. Sometimes worth is determined in the classroom. Report-card time. My worth is determined by how many As and Bs I've received. A lot of times, worth is determined by our peers. Whether you are a teenager or a middle-ager, who doesn't look around to see what their relative worth is compared to those around? Am I keeping up with the kid four lockers down from me? Am I keeping up with the Joneses four houses down from me?

What are you worth? And who would you trust to tell you?

Truth be told, when you come to church to get an answer to that question, it may feel and sound like you are getting somewhat of a mixed message. It is not long into most services where we in some way confess our sins. We remind God of how imperfect we are. We try to set the story straight as to what is really going on in our lives behind all the appearances. So in one sense the church tells you, or would have you believe, that you are not worth very much. You are a sinner. You are a broken human being in need of God's redemption.

And yet, on the other hand, the church also tells you that you are loved by none other than God himself. You are treasured so highly that God would empty himself, taking upon himself the flesh of humankind, and sacrificing himself upon the cross just for you. God so loved the world that he gave his only Son. This is how much you are worth.

So what is it? Am I a sinner—a struggling, broken human being—blemished in the eyes of God? Or am I the *imago dei*, the image of God, the one whom God loves so much he would sacrifice his life to redeem me? What is it?

Well, the answer is yes. To both questions the answer is yes.

And isn't that how you experience your life most of the time? Are there not those moments in your life when you see the amazing gifts God has given you, and you see within yourself the beauty with which you were created, when someone important to you has affirmed you for who you are or what you have done, and you say to yourself, maybe I am not so bad after all? But then because you know yourself better than most people do, you also have this view of your own shortcomings, the secret sins, the broken reality of your life, the things you know about yourself that if anybody else knew, you would die.

Maybe no truer words have been spoken than when the apostle Paul talks about how the gospel has been passed on to us to share with the world, and he puts it this way: "We have this treasure in clay jars." We know what he's talking about, don't we? We believe in the love and power of God, and yet we wonder, *What can the love and power of God do through me?* I may have this treasure, but I have it inside a clay jar. A clay soul. A clay body. A clay heart.

And so maybe we look to heaven and say, "What could a God like you do through a person like me?"

So the angels of God come to visit Abraham and Sarah and after some ancient Middle Eastern hospitality the angels turn to Abraham and they tell him that his ninety-year-old wife is going to have a son. Sarah is going to have a baby boy. And off in the background Sarah overhears their prophecy, and what does she do? She laughs. She laughs at the absurdity of the suggestion. That God could use an old woman like her. Had she not served her purpose? Had God not jerked her chain enough? Now ninety years old and God has got some big plans for her? Can God still use this chipped and cracked jar of clay? And God's response to her laughter is a question: "Is anything too wonderful for the Lord?"

Now, that is a question for us to ponder for a moment. And maybe we might want to ask it another way: Is there anything too wonderful that God could not do it through me? That's really what Sarah is wondering. That's really what she's laughing at: the possibility that God could have something wonderful still planned for her life, that this clay jar could possibly still hold some fine wine.

What possibilities are you entertaining? What wonderful things could you imagine God doing through you? Or have you already determined your worth? Have you already decided that this clay jar of yours is only capable of doing do so much?

I grew up in Detroit. Most of my friend's fathers worked on the assembly lines at Ford and Chrysler and GM. And the thing you learn about in Detroit—I don't know if it was really true, it might be urban legend—is when you go and buy a car, you find out what day it was assembled. And the trick was that you never bought a car that was assembled on Monday or Friday. Those were the days when people would call in sick in order to get a long weekend, and that meant the assembly line was apt to be a little shorthanded and who knows how your car got put together.

How did you get put together? Did God call in sick when you were assembled in your mother's womb? Or are you an instrument of God's design, through which God has planned to do something quite wonderful? Have you considered that God might have something so amazing planned for your life, that to even consider it, it could only make you laugh?

Are you laughing much these days? Are you laughing about the possibility that God might use you in some incredible way? Or has the thought never passed through your mind?

Do you remember that scene in *Mary Poppins* where Bert and Mary Poppins and the two children go visit Uncle Albert, and good old Uncle Albert is up on the ceiling laughing? And his laughing caused him to rise up there in the first place. As soon as the others start to laugh, it causes them to float as well. Before you know it, the whole gang is up there having a tea party because they are laughing, but you had to laugh before you could rise.

I wonder about that when it comes to you and me. I wonder if within us there are not some frequent stirrings of possibility that God places within our soul, and if we were to consider the possibility that God might do something so wonderful through us, it would make us laugh. But, you see, you have to laugh before you can rise, before you can rise to the task that God might have in store for you.

The Bible is filled with hilarious people. You can just hear them laughing! Moses being called to Egypt; you've got to be kidding me. David fighting Goliath? Not a chance. Isaiah the man of unclean lips . . . the prophet of God? No way. A virgin conceiving the Messiah? It's just not going to happen. Peter and Andrew, James and John—fishers of men? Yeah, right. Paul the Pharisaical zealot . . . now the missionary to the Gentiles? It just can't be. If you didn't laugh you would cry! Jars of clay, all of them. Filled with the new wine of God's great plan and possibility.

In New Jersey there are a few folks who know about a guy named Lee Schmookler. That's a tough name to go through life with. Lee Schmookler was leading a pretty good life. At age thirty-four he was a successful businessman and a part-time football coach. But when Lee was thirty-four, someone introduced him to gambling. He started playing cards, placing bets, going to the track and the casino. And it became an obsession, an addiction. He emptied the family bank account, lost his job, and lost his wife and family. And he ended up homeless and wandering the Atlantic City boardwalk begging for money—not to eat, but to gamble.

Just after his second suicide attempt a fellow vagrant pointed him to the Atlantic City Rescue Mission, and what he found there were people whose only interest was to love him. He found a God who loved him and a God who had a plan for his life. And he learned about the Holy Spirit and his power to help him battle his gambling addiction. After a time Lee felt the call to do what had been done for him: to help people without food and shelter, and to work with people gripped with addictions.

It wasn't long before Lee Schmookler became the head of the Newark City Rescue Mission, and it wasn't long before he was leading a ministry that served seventeen hundred meals a day to the poor, counseled 100 men daily struggling with addiction, and housed 150 men nightly in emergency shelter. If you would have asked Lee Schmookler, successful businessman, if he would someday be serving seventeen hundred meals a day to the poor, he would have laughed. If you would have asked Lee Schmookler, hopeless gambling addict staggering on the Atlantic City boardwalk, if he would someday be responsible for counseling 100 addicts at a time and sheltering 150 homeless at a time, more peals of laughter.

But you see, there is no clay jar that God cannot fill with his new wine of spirit and purpose. And when they asked Lee Schmookler about his life he said, "God takes a Jewish white guy from the Bronx, and sends him to make Christians in a rescue mission in Newark—now that's a God with a sense of humor."

You see, you have to laugh before you can rise.

Have you been disqualified from the incredible possibilities of God? And if you have, who disqualified you? "Oh, but you don't understand, Reverend. I'm too old." Says who? "I'm too young." According to whom? "I'm too busy." Who said so? "I'm too infirmed." Do you have a doctor's note? "I'm not a good enough person." Who's the judge of that?

Several years ago in Pittsburgh there was a prolonged steel strike. Management and the union were miles apart in their demands, and it looked like the industry would remain at a standstill for months. A steelworker named Dave Griffith couldn't take it anymore. He felt like God was telling him that it was up to him, a lowly steelworker, to do something about it. So Dave walked into the negotiating room one day, uninvited, and he pled for the two sides to reconcile their differences for the sake of the people of western Pennsylvania. Not long after that, the strike was settled.

Now, for a man to get the courage to do something that bold is one thing. But when the man is a severe stutterer, mortified to talk in front of groups of people . . . to stand there and stutter and stammer in the effort to plead for reconciliation—that is a person who has not allowed himself to be disqualified from the possibilities. Later, when asked why the warring factions had listened to Dave Griffith's stuttered plea, one of the executives responded, "Nobody with a stutter like that can step into such a ticklish situation like that on his own power. God had to be in it." Just a clay jar filled with new wine. It's really quite laughable.

I don't know what is stirring within your heart. I don't know if you have a feeling or a passion to respond to some human need. Maybe you have a heart for the poor, or for children, or for the hungry, or for the outcasts, or for the environment, or for peace in the world . . . or maybe nothing at all is stirring within you, which would be too bad. But has you ever reached the point where you've chuckled to yourself? Have you considered the outlandish possibility that nothing is too wonderful that God could not do it through you?

I can't wait to put our chipped and cracked jars of clay together and let the new wine of the Spirit fill us, and do something outlandish to make a difference in this part of the world. God would want nothing less.

"We have this treasure," writes the apostle, "in clay jars, so that it may be made clear that this extraordinary power belongs to God and does not come from us."

WHEN LIFE GOES AGAINST YOU

Jeremiah 23:5–8

LIFE, THEY SAY, is a matter of how you look at it.

The story is told of an old man named Morris and his wife, Sadie. Morris was an old man in his final days in the hospital, and his wife Sadie was there by his side. Morris looked up at Sadie and said to her, "Do you remember, Sadie, how when we were young and just married and we opened up that little shop in Kiev, but the Cossacks came in and drove us out, and you were right there by my side?"

"Oh yes," said Sadie, "I remember."

Said Morris: "And remember how we moved to Berlin and I opened up that little butcher shop, but the Nazis came and drove us out, and you were right there by my side?"

"Of course," said Sadie, "I remember, Morris."

Said Morris: "And then remember how we moved to the Bronx and we opened up that little dry goods place, but then the gangs came and drove us out, and you were right there by my side?"

"Yes, yes," said Sadie, "I remember."

Said Morris: "And then remember how we moved down here to Miami and I had my heart attack, and you were right there by my side?"

"How could I forget?" said Sadie.

"Sadie," said Morris, "now that I'm close to the end of my life, there is something I've always wanted to say to you."

"What is it, dear Morris?" said Sadie.

"Sadie," said Morris, "I think you're a jinx."

Life is a matter of how you look at it.

Sparky was the name given to a young boy who grew up in St. Paul, Minnesota, some eighty years ago. The boy was a very shy boy. Very intelligent—but painfully shy. His mother, for example, helped him make valentines for his grade school class, but his shyness kept him from passing them out, so he brought them home that afternoon. He tried his hand at drawing and even enrolled in a correspondence school. He was mediocre, receiving a C in the drawing of children. His drawings for his high school yearbook were turned down. He fell in love with a redhead, but his proposal for marriage was rejected. His mother died when he was twenty.

So what do you do with a life like that? If you're Charles Schulz, you turn all that painful childhood into a comic strip and call it *Peanuts* and become the most famous cartoonist in the world.

Life is a matter of how you look at it.

Some called him a holy man. Some called him a prophet. Some called him a troublemaker. But whatever you called him, Jeremiah was a man who lived in a bad time. That's the only thing you could call it: a bad time. It was a time that out-recessed the recession, out-depressed the Depression, and out-crashed the crash. It was a bad time. Israel—the great nation of Israel—had been sacked. The great power of Babylon and its king Nebuchadnezzar had swooped into Palestine and nearly leveled the city of Jerusalem. Laid it to ruins. Not only that, but dragged off most of its people back to Babylon, where they were to be held in exile for the course of four generations. It was a bad time. Some wondered if Jeremiah, who had foreseen some of these events, might not even be the jinx. There was nothing good about what was going on, no light at the end of the tunnel, no hope for a brighter day.

Maybe you've lived in a time like that. Maybe you are living in a time like that now. Maybe you've lost your job—you are a part of the percentages they tell us who don't have a job, and you are not getting any of your calls returned. Maybe you are struggling to hold on to your home. You can't afford your mortgage any longer, and you don't know where the next payment is coming from. Maybe you are battling some bad health—the direction of your illness is not heading in the right way—and you're not sure that the doctor knows what to do. Maybe you are having problems in your marriage. You can't seem to get on the same page, your feelings are changing, you're worried about your partner's unfaithfulness. Or maybe it's your children. One or more of them have you worried and you don't know what to do. You got that call that no parent wants to get. It doesn't take much for life to feel like it's going against you—like the armies of Babylon are at the gate.

But life is a matter of how you look at it. And so there is old Jeremiah standing in the ruin streets of Jerusalem, buildings still smoldering. Mount Zion flattened. The headlines of the *Jerusalem Gazette* exclaiming, "All Is Lost." And the holy man, the troublemaker, the prophet stands forth and says to the people—the people left behind as well as the people sent into exile—"The days are surely coming, says the Lord, when I will fulfill the promise I made to the house of Israel and the house of Judah. In those days and at that time I will cause a righteous Branch to spring up for David; and he shall execute justice and righteousness in the land. In those days Judah will be saved and Jerusalem will live in safety."

Life is a matter of how you look at it.

Jeremiah looked at life through the lens of a promise—the promise that God had made to Israel that he would love her to the end, that he would never abandon Israel, that he would be faithful no matter what—that despite the evidence to the contrary, despite the fact that Jerusalem was a pile of ruins, despite the appearances that maybe God had in fact abandoned Israel, Jeremiah never let go of the promise. "Someday," he said, "someday, a righteous branch will spring up. Judah will be saved, and Jerusalem will live in safety."

Life is a matter of how you look at it.

Think of what we do at Christmastime. In the church we call it Advent, which is a very strange time. We spend a lot of time in Advent dressing things up and putting the best face on things. Decorations are coming out. Wreaths are hung. Lights are going up outside the house. Music is playing. The world puts on a happy costume. And there is good reason to do so: to celebrate something we believe has happened, that the light of the world has come into the world, that God so loved the world that he gave his only Son. Peace on earth and good will toward all. It's all good.

We put on our happy costume, even if we are never quite sure what we are happy about. In fact, we are never quite sure if we are happy at all.

Strangely, every year at the beginning of Advent we see fights breaking out across the nation—on Black Friday. People wrestling over the last remaining super-duper-deluxe toy. Someone who cut in line at the cash register. Someone whose kid didn't get a chance to sit in Santa's lap. Maybe you saw the stories of those who wished they could have stood in line to buy their child a toy, but there is no money. There's hardly enough even to buy food. Or the story of the widow whose first Christmas without her husband is this Christmas, and she just can't bring herself to be happy. Or the soldier a half of a world away who is tired of the patrols and the fear and the shooting. He just wants to come home. The list goes on, and while we put on the costume of happiness, the truth of the matter is that we may not be really sure what we are happy about or even if we are happy.

But of course that's what the gospel is about. The good news is for people who don't have their lives together. Advent is for people who have something missing, for people who look around them and see ruin, for people who wonder if they're jinxed. Advent if for people who need a promise. They don't need much, but they need a promise. They need to know that somehow God is going to make it better. He may not make it perfect. He may not make it exactly the way we want it to be. But the promise is that he is going to make it better.

And sometimes that's all you really need is just the promise. When a couple comes together in the front of the sanctuary and exchanges vows, they know that life is a crap shoot. They know that life sometimes will work with them and sometimes it will work against them. Sometimes it will be plenty, sometimes it will be want. Sometimes it will be sickness and sometimes it will be health. Sometimes it will be joy, and sometimes it will be sorrow. But all they want right now is a promise—a promise that come hell or high water, you will stick with me and I will stick with you.

When they baptize a baby, parents know that life has all sorts of tricks up its sleeve. And they don't know what those tricks are for their child. All they know and all they want their baby to know is that, no matter what, he or she is a child of the promise, the covenant. That, no matter what, God will never let her down, and Mom and Dad will never let her down. So when trouble comes, and trouble usually comes to all of us, there is someone to call, in heaven and on earth.

Sometimes all you need is a promise.

History is filled with people who waited on the promise, who believed that despite how life had gone against them, God was still for them. God still had a plan. God still had a purpose.

Cripple him and you have a Sir Walter Scott. Lock him in a prison cell and you have a John Bunyan. Bury him in the snows of Valley Forge and you have a George

Washington. Subject him to bitter religious prejudice and you have a Disraeli. Strike him down with polio and he becomes an FDR. Deafen him and you have Ludwig van Beethoven. Have him born black in the racist South and you have Martin Luther King Jr. Have him lose his job, fail in business, suffer a nervous breakdown, suffer defeat in a half dozen elections, and lose his own child—and what you have is Abraham Lincoln.

And all they needed was just a promise.

Do you remember the story of little eight-year-old Glenn Cunningham? He and his brother Floyd were caught in a fire inside his schoolhouse. His brother Floyd died. Little Glenn was badly burned, especially his legs. The doctors took one look and said they had to amputate. Little Glenn begged them not to, but they said they had to. But little Glenn said no, because little Glenn remembered a Bible verse he learned in Sunday school—from Isaiah 40: Those who wait upon the Lord shall renew their strength. They shall mount up with wings like eagles. They shall run and not be weary. They shall walk and not faint. That's all that little Glenn needed—just that promise. So the surgeon staid his scalpel. Little Glenn kept his legs. And God kept his promise, and little Glenn Cunningham set the world record in running the mile. Those who wait upon the Lord shall renew their strength. They shall mount up with wings like eagles. They shall run and not be weary. They shall walk and not faint.

Life is a matter of how you look at it. Sometimes, when the world is against you, all you need is a promise.

So the prophet steps forth—in the midst of the ruins, the smoldering city, the exiled community—and says, "The days are surely coming, says the Lord, when I will fulfill the promise I made to the house of Israel and to the house of Judah. . . . A righteous branch will spring up . . . one who shall execute justice and righteousness. . . . Judah will be saved . . . and Jerusalem will live in safety."

It is what the gospel is about, for those who need a way to look at life—life that may be against them. For those who are not quite sure what they are happy about, or if they are even happy to begin with. For those who need, more than anything else, just a promise.

For the promise has come. The promise is here. Rejoice. Emmanuel.

ᴛHE ꜰEAR OF ɢIANTS

Numbers 13:1–33

A WHILE AGO I found an article in the newspaper about an eight-year-old girl who lives up in the little town of Washburn, Wisconsin. Her name was Holly Driscoll, and Holly decided a while back that her elementary school really needed a van. Class trips and such would be a lot easier if the school owned a van. The adults told her, of course, that there was no money in the school budget for such a costly item as a van. But then Holly discovered that the Campbell Soup Company has a program whereby if you save enough of their soup labels you can redeem them for certain school-type things. Five hundred seventy-five labels will get you 12 boxes of crayons; 88,250 labels will get you an Apple computer; and 975,000 labels will get you a van. And so it is that Holly started to work saving soup can labels. Soon she got her friends saving labels, and pretty soon word got out to the outlying areas . . . and before you know it, the whole state is saving labels for Holly Driscoll's school van. At last count they had 30,000 labels, only 945,000 labels to go. Asked if she thought the task was too monumental, Holly replied, "Naaah, I think we can do it."

When I read that article I remember thinking to myself that there was something about Holly Driscoll I liked very much. I do not know if she ever made it even close to her goal of 975,000 soup labels, but still there was something about Holly Driscoll that really, really impressed me. And I realized that what so impressed me about Holly Driscoll was that here was a little eight-year-old girl faced with a monumental task of saving 975,000 soup labels, and chances are that she had been told by a thousand adults that she couldn't do it, that there was no way she was going to get even close to getting that school van—and yet she was still doing it. What impressed me about Holly Driscoll was that, despite the prevailing opinion, she went out to slay the giant.

Twenty years ago a young Canadian boy by the name of Terry Fox woke up one morning with a sharp pain in his leg. Soon he found out that it was bone cancer and that his right leg needed to be amputated right above the knee. The night before his surgery he had a dream that he would run across Canada from shore to shore. He never forgot that dream. Later he told his friends and his family, and they all said it was a nice idea, but it would never happen. He only had one leg. You can't run across Canada with one leg.

Months after his amputation, along with a well-fitting prosthesis, Terry began training, working up to thirteen and a half miles a day—a day! In April 1980 he began his marathon. It was going to be a marathon to raise money for cancer research. He asked people to pledge money for his run across Canada. He dipped his artificial leg into the Atlantic up in Newfoundland and started his run. He averaged twenty-eight to thirty miles a day, but the first one thousand miles not many people noticed. But Terry kept running anyway, and soon people could see that this kid was for real. And all of a sudden pledges began to pour in with every mile that Terry ran. People crowded the streets of the small towns through which he ran. After five months Terry Fox had put thirty-three hundred miles behind him, but that's when he started to cough and get weak. He kept on going, but the cough got worse and the legs got weaker—and then they found cancer in Terry's lungs. This time they couldn't stop it. But neither could they stop all those pledges from coming in. They just kept coming. Months later Terry Fox lost his battle to cancer, but not without raising $22 million for cancer research.

Despite the prevailing opinion, despite being told by everybody he knew that he couldn't do it, Terry Fox went out to slay the giant.

Lord knows there are a lot of giants in this world. We are surrounded by giants. Pick up the newspaper and you soon discover that there are giants everywhere. There are giants in New York City. There are giants in the Middle East, North Korea, and West Africa. There are giants all over our own country—with names like poverty and hunger, AIDS and cancer, crime and racism and violence. There are monsters all over the place. Maybe a giant is living real close to you, and it's not a friendly giant. Maybe a giant is living in your school, your home, or your heart. Yes, there are all kinds of giants walking around this world—and the question that gets asked again and again is, "Who's going to slay the giant?"

I don't know about you, but I don't think of myself as a giant slayer. I'd like to think of myself as a giant avoider. I'd just as soon stay out of the way of these giants and keep out of their paths. Even better, I'd like to pretend that they're not there. You know, maybe if I don't look—if I don't acknowledge that these giants are really there, then maybe they might go away. Kind of like when you were a kid and staying under the covers to keep the monsters from coming. That seems to me to be a pretty good way to deal with the giants walking around this world.

And I don't suppose that feeling is too different from the story in Numbers 13—the story of the people of Israel as they are approaching the land of Canaan, just at the edge of the promised land, the place toward which they had been wandering through the wilderness. Moses, like a good general, sends out spies to find out what this land of Canaan is all about. And so the spies go and come back, and they report to the people of Israel that giants live in the land of Canaan. And that there was no chance that the people of Israel would ever inhabit the land of Canaan, because there were giants in that land, and, in fact, the giants were so big that—and this is what they said—"To ourselves we seemed like grasshoppers."

Understand what is happening here. The spies of Israel had allowed the size of these giants to determine in their own minds what size they were. Think about that for a moment. "To ourselves we seemed like grasshoppers."

As I've said, I don't see myself as a giant slayer. I wonder if I have allowed the giants of this world to determine in my own mind what size I really am. And I wonder if we are all doing the same thing—if, in our fear of giants, in our fear of all the monumental tasks and problems out in the world, we have allowed the size of the giants to determine our own size. "To ourselves we seemed like grasshoppers."

As the rest of the story goes—among those spies there was a man named Caleb—and Caleb had a different opinion. He gathered the people together and offered what Presbyterians might call a "minority report." Caleb did not dispute the size of the giants. He did not say to the people that these giants were not as big as these other guys said they were. Nor did Caleb try to deny the existence of these giants. He did not say that maybe the hot sun made them seem so big, or that when we attack maybe they won't be there. Caleb says nothing of the sort. Instead, Caleb said, "Let us go up at once and occupy the land, for we are well able to overcome it." That's a different attitude.

It's not that the giants didn't exist, or that they weren't as big; Caleb just refused to let the size of the giants determine his own size. No talk of grasshoppers from the mouth of Caleb. He knew that he was a lot bigger than what those giants made him out to be.

And so I wonder that if there is any chance of God using us in this world—if there is any chance of you and I making a difference in the world for the sake of the kingdom of God, if there is any chance of slaying the giants and inhabiting the land—it all might need to begin with you and me taking a whole new look at ourselves.

About thirty years ago the Japanese city of Sapporo opened its brand-new subway, but over the course of time they were sad to report that over sixty people had used the subway to end their lives by jumping in front of the trains. More than sixty people had found no way to escape the giants.

A few years ago someone got the idea to install mirrors in all the subway stations—floor to ceiling and wall to wall. The mirrors were put there, of course, so that people could have one last look before they jumped. Years passed before someone jumped again.

I wonder if, before you and I conclude that we are much too small for the giants around us, we need to take another look at ourselves. I wonder if it might not be a good idea, before we give ourselves up to these giants, to take a look into the mirror and see what we see.

What I hope you see in that mirror—when you take the time to look—is two things. First I hope you see the incredible creation of God, a person whom God has had his mind on since the beginning of creation. I hope you see in that mirror a person to whom God has given incredible gifts—a person for whom God has an incredible purpose—a person who is in this world to slay giants no matter their size. I hope you see in that mirror a person whom the psalmist says is just one notch below the angels.

Daryl Potter, a native of England who now lives in Canada, tells of a day several years ago when she was working in her office and she banged her knee against a filing cabinet. That little bump on her knee ended up turning into something called thrombophlebitis, and from there her life began to fall apart. Her illness led from one thing to another, and she was forced to endure scores of operations that led to the amputation of three of her four limbs. She lost the sight of one eye. During this terrible pilgrimage she became addicted to pain medication and lost her husband. What remained were her three children, one healthy limb, and one healthy eye. It may be hard to believe that Daryl is the author of a book titled *God's Wonderful Gift to Me*. And in it she writes,

> It is not my missing limbs that matter now, but what is within me that counts. I feel like a painting on an easel. So often I will try to jump off that easel and paint myself. But if I can stay on that easel I know God will paint a perfect picture of me, one I could never be ashamed of, a picture so perfect that I will be able to withstand anything, no matter how bad it may be at the time. God's gift to me is life, and it is what I do with this life that will be my gift to God.

So the first thing I hope you see in that mirror is a person whom God created and is still creating—a person whom God put here not for the giants to slay, but to slay the giants.

But that's not the only thing I hope you see in the mirror. I hope you also see Jesus—no matter where you are, no matter what you might think of yourself, no matter how big the giants might be. When you look in the mirror and wonder to yourself if you are big enough for the task ahead of you, I hope that what you see is not just yourself but the God of heaven.

We all know the wonderful story of David and Goliath. David, the little shepherd boy—the youngest son of Jesse—and Goliath, the giant Philistine. The entire army of Israel is paralyzed in fear of this giant. They know how big he is, and they have allowed his size to determine how small they are. But little David grabs his slingshot and his five smooth stones, and he walks out there to square off with the giant. And David says to the giant, "You come to me with sword and spear and javelin, but I come to you in the name of the Lord of Hosts."

You see, David had looked in the mirror, and what he saw was not just himself but the Lord of Hosts. And when you know the Lord of Hosts is with you, there isn't a giant too big in this land that can't be slain.

When I was a little boy I cut the bottom of my foot on a piece of dirty glass. My father told me I had to go to the doctor's office to get a tetanus shot. I don't know about you, but getting shots is not my most favorite thing in the world. I hate shots. I hate even the sight of a needle. But I was a brave little buckaroo; I didn't make much of a fuss. My dad took me down to the doctor's office, and we took our seats there in the waiting room. I remember sitting there trying to look as brave as can be. I had that look on my face that said, "No problem!" But when the nurse came out and called my name, my father leaned over and asked, "Do you want me to go in with you?" And I said, "Well, if you want." So he did.

As we sat there in the examining room I began to smell pain. When little children go into doctor's offices, they smell pain. So there I was smelling pain, and just before the doctor came in to give me the shot, my father said to me, "When the doctor comes in, the first thing you're going to want to do is look at that needle in his hand. But I don't want you to look at that needle. I don't even want you looking at the doctor. I want you to look right at me." I nodded yes with a stiff upper lip.

The doctor came in a second later, and the first thing I looked at was that needle, which was at least a foot and a half long. Then I looked at the doctor, and not only did the doctor smell like pain, he looked like pain. And then I remembered to look at the other person in the room, my father. And the smile on his face took the edge off my fear just enough to endure that shot. It still hurt, but the needle didn't seem as big anymore.

So what would the likes of Caleb and young David and Daryl Potter and legions of others have us know? Wherever you go, wherever you may be, and whomever you may face, Jesus is always in the room with you. The Lord of Hosts. The King of Heaven. And there is nothing that you and Jesus cannot do together. There is no task that you and he cannot accomplish. There is no giant that you cannot slay.

I so love the story that Robert Louis Stevenson often told about a ship that was at the mercy of a violent storm. The ship was being tossed back and forth, and the crew was paralyzed with fear. Finally a sailor working far down in the hull of the ship could stand it no longer. He stumbled up the stairs and made his way into the control room. There he saw the captain of the ship grappling with the controls—fighting to navigate the ship along the rocky coastline. As the young sailor stood there, the captain looked over his shoulder and spotted the petrified sailor, and when he saw the fear in the sailor's eyes, the captain smiled. With that the sailor made his way back down to the hull of the ship. When the rest of the crew asked him whether they were going to make it, the sailor said, "We're going to be just fine." They asked him how he knew. The sailor replied, "I know, because I've seen the face of the captain, and he smiled at me."

Folks, there are a lot of giants out there, and a lot of them are pretty big and pretty close. We can spend the rest of our lives trying to avoid these giants, but I don't think that's what God wants us to do. God didn't create us to be grasshoppers; he created us to be his children. And as his children it might do us good to look in the mirror again, for there we might see the face of the person whom God created as well as the face of the person whom God sent. And maybe, just maybe, we will see him smile. Maybe we can hear him say, "In this world you will have troubles, but be of good cheer, for I have overcome the world." The good news is that there is no giant that those two people can't slay.

$\mathcal{I}$T $\mathcal{M}$ATTERS

Mark 2:13–17

ON JUNE 8, 1941, ONE of the greatest sermons ever delivered, in my humble opinion, was delivered at Oxford University Church of St. Mary the Virgin in Oxford,
England. It was delivered, you'll be surprised to hear, by C. S. Lewis. If I had been
there I doubt I could have understood it. You have to read it about five times to really
get the full weight of what he is saying, and I've probably read it fifty times since the
first time. It's a sermon called "The Weight of Glory," and you can pick it up at the
local bookstore or order it online.

It's a sermon about the meaning and purpose of life—why were we born and
what our destiny is. Ultimately, Lewis writes, we who have been born in the image of
God are longing to receive the glory of God—and the glory of God comes when he
says to us in the end, "Well done, good and faithful servant." That's what we most long
for: to come face to face with God and hear him say, "Well done, good and faithful
servant." That is the case for every human being. In fact, Lewis writes that each of us
is truly an eternal being, and that our destiny is toward one of two places: heaven or
hell. Every single person you meet, he says, is a person you have an impact upon in
their journey to one place or the other. We are either helping people to heaven, or we
are helping them to hell.

Lewis ends his sermon this way:

> It is a serious thing to live in a society of possible gods and goddesses,
> to remember that the dullest and most uninteresting person you
> can talk to may one day be a creature which, if you say it now,
> you would be strongly tempted to worship, or else a horror and

a corruption such as you now meet, if at all, only in a nightmare. All day long we are, in some degree, helping each other to one or other of these destinations. It is in the light of these overwhelming possibilities, it is with the awe and the circumspection proper to them, that we should conduct all our dealings with one another, all friendships, all loves, all play, all politics. There are no ordinary people. You have never talked to a mere mortal. Nation, cultures, arts, civilizations—these are mortal, and their life is to ours as the life of a gnat. But it is immortals whom we joke with, work with, marry, snub, and exploit—immortal horrors or everlasting splendours. Next to the Blessed Sacrament itself, your neighbor is the holiest object presented to your senses.

"There are no ordinary people. You have never talked to a mere mortal. . . . It is immortals whom we joke with, work with, marry, snub, and exploit."

Jesus knew about this, I think. It seems that just about every time Jesus turns around in the Gospels, he is pausing before a human being. And the reason he is pausing is that he sees something that we don't often see. He sees an immortal. He sees someone who is on his way or her way to eternity—immortal horror or everlasting splendor, as Lewis would say it. Jesus never sees an ordinary human being.

The exchange we read in those three verses from the Gospel of Mark almost say it all. Jesus is hanging out with Levi and his friends—fellow tax collectors and non-religious people. And the Pharisees detect this unusual gathering—a supposed holy rabbi hanging around with the common folk: the nonreligious folk, the underclass, or worse, "the sinners." That's what the Pharisees call them—the sinners. And sinners were not folks the Pharisees thought worthy of concern. The sinners were the disregarded ones.

But Jesus regards them. Jesus pauses before them. Jesus takes a meal with them. Because, Jesus says, there are no ordinary people. These are immortals in our midst. It matters what I do when I am in their presence. I can encourage them one way or the other. It matters what I do.

Does it matter what you do? Does it matter what you do when you brush shoulders with the immortals in your midst? I'm not just talking about the big things; I'm talking maybe even more of the small things. Does it matter how you regard the unordinary people who cross your path? Does it matter how you relate to people who are not interesting to you—or, even worse, people who seem to be an impediment to you? It can be a startling thing when you realize that you have actually come to see some people in your life as an impediment.

It's certainly a startling thing to see in the story we read out of 1 Kings about Ahab and Jezebel, king and queen of Israel. Ahab has his sights on a vineyard next to his palace in Jezreel, but a man named Naboth owns the vineyard, a family treasure that has been passed down to him through the generations. But the king wants the vineyard so that he can turn it into a vegetable garden; it would just be perfect for him. Ahab even makes Naboth a deal—a great deal. Ahab will give Naboth an even better garden if he can just have his garden. But Naboth says no. And when Naboth says no, Naboth becomes an impediment. No longer a neighbor—now an impediment. Jezebel gets word of Ahab's disappointment and pouting and says, "What's the problem? You're the king. Treat him for what he is: an impediment!" And as the story goes, Jezebel conspires to have Naboth killed, all because he owned the wrong garden at the wrong place at the wrong time. It's never good to own the wrong garden at the wrong place at the wrong time.

Do you see what happens to us sometimes? We see the immortals, the eternal beings, the unordinary people in our midst often not for what they are, which is everlasting splendors, but for what they pose for us as: impediments, obstacles, someone in the way.

I went out to dinner with some friends years ago. It was a little celebration we were hoping to have. We went to a restaurant I've never been to. We sat and we ordered. And then we waited. We waited. We waited. We didn't have all night to spend there, but evidently someone in the kitchen thought we did. So every time the waitress—a young woman, twenty years old maybe—came by, we asked about the food. "It will be a few minutes," she said. We looked around, and there was no food at any of the tables. Something had gone badly wrong in the kitchen, something clearly outside the waitress's control.

But that didn't seem to matter as to how I regarded her. She became for me the representative of the problem. She became the impediment to my full stomach—the detour to my next commitment. And I treated her so. It's not that I was rude. I just didn't take into consideration that this was likely one of the worst nights of her life, much worse than mine. I didn't imagine the tears that were likely to pour out of her when she got home, the confusion over trying to do the best job she could and receiving in response the anger of hungry, impatient diners. For me and the others, she became mortal, and our disregard likely killed a little bit of her spirit. We wanted the vineyard, but she wouldn't and couldn't give us the vineyard.

Years ago a young woman came to see me about a struggle she was having. We talked about a lot of things during our sessions, including her job; she was a check-out cashier in the local grocery store. At one point she said something that's never left me. She said, "You'd be amazed what people do when they come through the checkout line. You'd be amazed at how they behave. And you would be amazed at how few of them look at me. Most people will not make eye contact with me. They will not regard me. It is as if I'm not there." And then she said, "You would be surprised, Reverend, how many of them are in your congregation."

It matters what you do. There are no ordinary people. You have never talked to a mere mortal.

It's been about twenty-five years since Robert Fulghum published his best-selling little book *All I Needed to Know I Learned in Kindergarten.* It sold like hotcakes. Book critics panned it for its triteness and saccharine perspective, as if life could be that simple. And it's true that life's never that simple. But that doesn't mean Fulghum's book isn't true. And it's true because what you're learning about in kindergarten is what it means to be human, and what it means to regard other humans.

Among the things Fulghum learned in kindergarten:

1. Share everything.
2. Play fair.
3. Don't hit people.
4. Put things back where you found them.
5. Clean up your own mess.
6. Don't take things that aren't yours.
7. Say you're sorry when you hurt someone.

The list goes on, but what the list doesn't say is that which is most important to say and which is the premise to life itself. None of these things matter if we don't see ourselves for who we are: the children of God eternally destined. Then it matters what we do. We are helping each other to either one or another of the destinations!

Fifty years ago Edward Lorenz, the meteorologist, was using a numerical computer model in trying to come up with a long-term weather forecast. When he was rerunning the model, instead of using a factor of .506127 he took a shortcut and used .506 instead, a minuscule variation. The result was a drastically different forecast. He realized that just a slight variation of factors significantly changes the outcome. That's where the butterfly effect comes from—that the flap of a butterfly's wings over Brazil can cause a tornado over Texas. Every motion, every action, every gesture sets into motion a different set of events. It matters what we do. One thing leads to another, leads to another.

So the grimace the customer makes at the table, or the disregard the checkout girl perceives, or the deadly covetousness of a garden, or the lunch with the tax collectors—each and all set into motion the path that people take either to heaven or hell.

It matters what we do.

Do you know the story of Donald Driver? Donald Driver grew up in Houston and from an early age was trouble. In seventh grade he learned from his brother the art of stealing cars. At age twelve he became a professional car thief. Donald Driver would steal car after car, night after night. He did it to get money to support his family, which had been living in the back of a U-Haul truck. Donald Driver was a banged-up boy. But then one night he banged up someone else. He had just started up another one of his stolen cars when he heard sirens. In his haste to escape he didn't notice the old woman backing her car out of her driveway. He broadsided her, going very, very fast. He jumped out of his demolished car and started sprinting. But something told him to go back and check the old woman. When he did he found her all right, but by that time the police were almost on him. He looked at the woman, and then he looked at the approaching police cars. And that's when he heard the old woman say, "You go sit on my porch." And Driver did.

When the police came they asked, "Who's that on your porch swing?"

"Oh," she said, "that's my grandson." When the police had gone the old woman walked up to the porch and told the young Driver to get into her house, and that's where she tore him up one side and down the other and told him that this was his chance to turn his life around.

Did he turn his life around? No, not right away. But that one gesture of grace, of love, of caring dogged him until he realized that maybe the old woman was right—maybe there was more to his life than crime. The rest, they say, is history.

Today Donald Driver is a star receiver for the Green Bay Packers. He steals foot-balls out of mid-air. But the amazing thing is that now he's not only a star receiver, he holds the record for the Green Bay Packers for the most community service appear-ances. He holds the record for the most honorarium dollars that go into the Donald Driver Foundation that is used to help people in need. He's loved by the fans, an all-around great guy. And do you know what else he does? He keeps making trips back to Houston, because that's where the old Donald Driver lived—the car thief. He goes back there to visit the woman he calls Grandma Johnson, the woman who saved his life—the woman who loved him first and then asked questions later, who regarded him, who saw him as an everlasting splendor. An unordinary human being.

It matters. Yes, it matters what we do.

THE THINGS WE GET TO DO

John 10:11–18

STUART HAMPLE AND Eric Marshall several years ago published a little book titled *Children's Letters to God*—a compilation of real children's letters to God. It's a tiny little book that doesn't take you more than five minutes to read through, but it is filled with wise and innocent and honest wonderments about God, the kinds of questions that children are less afraid to ask of God than adults.

For example: Lucy writes, "Dear God, Are you really invisible or is that just a trick?"

Anita writes, "Dear God, Is it true my father won't get in Heaven if he uses his Bowling Words in the house?"

From Jane: "Dear God, Instead of letting people die and having to make new ones, why don't you just keep the ones you got now?"

From Nan: "Who draws the lines around the countries?"

Neil writes, "Dear God, I went to this wedding and they kissed right in church. Is that OK?"

From Donny: "Dear God, Is Reverend Coe a friend of yours, or do you just know him through business?"

From Joyce: "Dear God, Thank you for the baby brother but what I asked for was a puppy."

From Peter: "Dear God, Please send Dennis Clark to a different camp this year."

And from Larry: "Maybe Cain and Abel would not kill each so much if they had their own rooms. It works with my brother."

Out of the mouths of babes. Children, I suppose, allow themselves, more than adults, to wonder out loud about God. If you were once a parent of a young child, you remember the endless stream of questions about God. It usually started with something innocuous, "Mommy, where did the leaf come from?" The leaf came from the tree. "Where did the tree come from?" The tree came from a seed. "Where did the seed come from?" The seed came from God. "And where did God come from?" Go ask your father.

Ever since we were young we have wanted to know about God.

A prominent Presbyterian preacher tells the story of a young couple he knew who had a four-year-old and a new baby whom they had brought home from the hospital. And one day the four-year-old asked the parents if she could have just a couple of minutes alone with the new baby. The baby was up in her crib. The parents looked at each other not knowing what plan might be afoot. But out of curiosity they let their daughter have her couple of minutes alone—not without, of course, following quietly behind and peeking in the door to make sure all was well. And what they saw was their four-year-old daughter standing on a chair and leaning over the crib, and what they heard her say to the baby was, "Tell me everything you know about God. I'm already starting to forget."

So in our lesson this morning, Jesus is teaching his disciples, and he says to them that he is the good shepherd. Inasmuch as the Gospel of John has worked hard to help us understand that Jesus is the Word of God made flesh, that Jesus is the Messiah of God come to deliver his people, that Jesus is the incarnation of God who reveals the very nature of God, now Jesus speaks of himself. For us who since we were children have been wanting to know about God, Jesus now teaches us that he is the good shepherd. "I am the good shepherd. I know my own and my own know me."

This is an amazing way to think of God. It is one thing for us to postulate ontologically about the existence of a Creator—someone or something that stood at the beginning of time and somehow made the seed that made the tree that made the leaf. It's another thing to wonder like little children what kind of God is God really like. But it is entirely another thing for us to hear Jesus say that he—the incarnate Word of God—is the good shepherd, who knows his own and his own know him.

In the Bible when the word "know" is used, or the word "knowledge," it speaks of something different than what we are used to thinking about when we think of knowing or knowledge. There are two kinds of knowledge. The first kind of knowledge is what I would call "Google knowledge." Google knowledge is knowledge you get from looking up things, Googling things. It's knowledge you get from a Wikipedia article. It is knowledge about something. I know the starting lineup of the St. Louis Cardinals. I know the sixty-six books of the Bible. I know the names of my neighbors. I know the life story of C. S. Lewis. You can Google these things and find them out for yourself.

The other kind of knowledge—the one the Bible refers to a great deal—is the knowledge that comes from relationship and intimacy. You can *know about* someone, and you can also *know* someone. Knowing about and knowing are two different things. When you are dating someone, you are in that stage of knowing about them. When you are celebrating your fiftieth anniversary, you can say you know them. A lot of people may know about you from your work or your neighborhood or your church, but probably only a few people know you—maybe even just one best friend. They've seen you at your best and worst. They have heard your faith and your doubt. They have celebrated your strength and endured your weakness. And they know you. You have been in relationship. You have achieved a level of intimacy.

It is no surprise that the gospel starts out with a story about Mary and Joseph and the conception of Jesus outside of marital relations. Joseph, because he doesn't really know much "about" anything, decides he is going to get out of this mess. But then he gets a visit from an angel who tells him that something is up. Matthew tells us that Joseph took Mary as his wife, but "knew her not" until she had the child. "Know" is the word for intimacy.

So Jesus the good shepherd says, "I know my own, and my own know me." Jesus the good shepherd says, I don't just know that I have "about" a hundred sheep in the flock, but I know my sheep well enough that I know when one has nibbled itself away, and I love that sheep enough that I leave the ninety-nine to find it.

The Pharisees and the Scribes knew a lot about God. They knew that God had a lot of laws and a lot of ways of doing things and a lot of commands. They knew a lot about God, yet they didn't know God.

But God comes in the person of Jesus for us to know and be known. God comes in the person of Jesus to be in relationship. God comes in the person of Jesus for us to have intimacy.

A lot of us Christians can run into the same difficulty, spending plenty of time and energy learning about God and even learning about Jesus—important information, to be sure—but when it comes to knowing God, being in relationship with God, and intimately connecting with God, we may be in that place where the shepherd knows us but we don't know the shepherd.

But knowing the shepherd is what the whole deal is about. The shepherd is the one who says to us, "I have come to give you life and give it to you abundantly." When we hear the call of Christ, the call of Christ is an invitation to come to know him. This is what Jesus invites us to do: come and know him. Jesus's call is not a call to do things, it is not a call to perform acts, it is not a call to run through a checklist of things to do. Rather, Jesus calls us to spend time with him so we can come to know him.

It was his call to the disciples. He called them to spend time with him, to walk with him, listen to him, hang out with the people he likes to hang out with, watch him as he does those things that showed what they meant to him.

When Jesus invites us into following him, it's all for the purpose of our knowing him, being in relationship with him, and growing intimately aware of him. And we want to know him. Our desire to do so comes out of our survey of the wondrous cross. "When I survey the wondrous cross on which the prince of glory died, my richest gain I count but loss, and pour contempt on all my pride." I see in the cross the good shepherd who lays down his life for the sheep. This is who God is. This is what God thinks about us. This is how far his love goes. I want to know him because of what I know about him. I want to spend time with him, because I want to be close to this love.

When we hear Christ call us, it is a call to draw close to this love, this abundant life.

When we hear the call to prayer, remember that prayer is not something we have to do, it is something we get to do. It is simply time with Jesus. Aquinas said that prayer "makes us the familiars of God." We pause to listen to what love has to say to us. We dwell in the presence of God. We grow familiar with God.

When Jesus calls us to read his word, remember that's it's not something we have to do, it's something we get to do. It's just time with Jesus. We sit at the feet of the one who loves us, and we listen to him loving us. When I was young and asked my parents to read me a book, half was because I wanted to hear the story, but the other half was because I wanted to hear their voices. I wanted to be with them. I wanted to know them.

When Jesus call us to serve the poor, it's not something we have to do, it's something we get to do. It is just an invitation to spend time with Jesus as he spends time with others. We come to know Jesus by hanging with the people he hangs with.

When Jesus tells us to forgive the one who has harmed us and love our enemy, it's not something we have to do, it's something we get to do. It is an invitation to join Jesus in the cross—to draw deeply from the grace and mercy of the cross, to know Christ crucified—so that we can sacrifice our own pride and stubbornness in order to participate more fully in the love of Christ.

When Jesus calls me to consider the lilies of the field, it's not something I have to do, it's something I get to do. It is an invitation for me to look and consider this incredible world that God has created around me and to realize that God loves me so much that he chose to make so many beautiful things for me to delight in. On top of it, I am invited to marvel that as much as he clothes the lilies of the field, how much more will he take care of us.

Isn't it interesting that we can turn these things we "get to do" into things we have to do?

Jesus tells that story of the man who throws the big party. He invites all these people, but they all have excuses—personal, business, recreation. For some reason they have gotten it into their minds that the party was somehow a chore to attend. The party-thrower says back to them, "It's a party, for gosh sakes. It's the chance for us to be together. All I'm inviting you to do is to be with me."

When I was an early teenager I remember my dad talking about a movie he wanted to take me to. It was some kind of nature movie, and because I was an early teenager with a certain need to be independent and untainted with anything that smelled of parents, I hemmed and hawed and put him off. Finally I told him that I needed to take a pass. Mind you, this is the guy who would have given his life for me, and spent a good bit of his life sacrificing for me to have what I needed. But I took a pass. I didn't need to go. And I remember the look on his face, though, when I said no. He was disappointed. He wasn't crushed, but he was disappointed. I'll never forget that look of disappointment. Now here's the thing: he wasn't disappointed because he couldn't go to the movie. He could go anytime he wanted. He's the one who had the car. He was disappointed because the movie was an excuse to be together—to spend time, to hang out—and for him to know me, and for me to know him.

How far we have fallen when the things we get to do turn into the things we have to do.

So the good shepherd calls us with that voice of love—not to the things we have to do, but to the things we get to do. None of the things that Jesus calls us to are what he needs us to do. It's just the reason to draw us close, to be with us, to share the intimacy of relationship. And to know, to really know.

Back to those children's letters to God. This one was from Nora. She writes, "Dear God, I don't ever feel alone anymore since I found you."

"I am the good shepherd," Jesus said. "I know my own and my own know me."

$\mathscr{F}$INISHING A $\mathscr{R}$ACE $\mathscr{D}$IFFERENT FROM THE $\mathscr{O}$NE $\mathscr{Y}$OU $\mathscr{S}$TARTED

Mark 1:16–20

I READ YEARS ago in the newspaper the story of a woman who lived outside of Cleveland, Ohio. Georgene had turned forty-two years old and wasn't happy about it. She decided she didn't want to look like a forty-two-year-old, and she got it into her mind to take up running. So she started running, first a little bit and then a little bit more. She got up to two miles a day and then three miles and then four miles. And she started feeling better about herself and less and less like a forty-two-year-old. Then she decided to give herself a little challenge and enter herself into a race.

She thought she might begin with a 10K, a ten-kilometer race, which is about six miles. The race was being held somewhere in Cleveland. When she arrived on the morning of the race, lots of folks were milling around. She heard on the speaker the announcement for the runners to assemble at the starting line. Georgene took her place. The gun went off, and Georgene, with this mass of runners, was off and running her first race.

She had seen the outline of the course before the race and knew that it was one of the courses that basically had the runners go out about three miles and then come back the remaining three miles. But Georgene noticed when they got to mile four they had not yet turned back and it didn't appear that they were going to. They were running a different course than what she thought. But when they got to mile seven Georgene knew that something was up. So she moved over close to another runner and asked, huffing and puffing, what happened to the finish line? "What finish line?" the fellow runner responded. "You're in the Cleveland Marathon! You've got nineteen more miles to go!" Turns out her 10K race was scheduled a half hour after the start of the marathon.

Georgene asked herself, *Should I stop or should I go on? No harm in going on, I suppose. Let's just see how far I can go. It's not the race I trained for. It's not the race I entered. But it is the race I'm in.* So she continued to run. And she ran. And she ran. And she ran. And she finished. "How could you finish this race for which you did not train?" the newspapers asked. Georgene said she started by taking it one mile at a time and then a half-mile at a time and then a quarter-mile at a time and then a few yards at a time and then, by the end, one step at a time.

She finished a race different from the one she started.

I want to wonder with you about finishing a race different, maybe, from the one you started.

I don't know where you are right now in your life. Each of us has been on the track for a certain amount of time. Some of us started a good while ago and have been around the track maybe more than we care to admit. Others have been on the track for a while, and still feel like they've got a good bit more to go. And some of you were put on the track not so long ago, and you feel like you are just getting started. Wherever you are in your life, you probably have it in your mind that you are in a certain race, and you have a certain ways to go.

The world will tell you that once you've been entered into a race, you don't have a whole lot of choice of joining another one. Geneticists will tell you that you were programmed a long time ago; your DNA was set, and you are who you are and you can't do much about it. Psychologists will tell you that you are largely a collection of your experiences and your family rearing, and that each of us carries around with us a certain amount of baggage. Sociologists will tell you that you are the product of your environment, and that you can take the person out of the neighborhood or the community, but you can't take the neighborhood or the community out of the person. Your parents may have mapped your life out for you—where you are going, your college and your profession. Others say that because of your age you are likely set in your ways, and there is no changing you now. Now that you are X years old, why, there is just no teaching an old dog new tricks.

The world wants to peg you. The world wants to get you to fit into some type of mold. The world wants to enter you into a certain race, and then tell you that the race you started is the race you have to finish.

I was teaching confirmation class a few years ago, and one of my students asked if he could come and see me. He told me that he was thinking about becoming a pastor and that he would like to learn more. So we talked. He went home. A couple of days later I got a call from his mother.

"We'll have none of that," she said.

"None of what?" I asked.

"I would very much appreciate you not talking to our boy about being a pastor." She made it sound like I was asking him to become an axe murderer.

"I don't understand," I said.

"You're right," she said. "You don't understand. His father and I already know what he's going to be. He's going to be an engineer. So don't go messing up his mind." He was in the race, and there was no other race for him to run.

So I want to know something. No matter where you are, no matter what race you're in, is it still possible for you to finish a race different from the one you started?

One of the things I love about the Bible is that it is filled with story after story about people who start one race and finish a different one—people whose lives have a before and an after, sometimes even lots of befores and lots of afters. People who thought life had to be one thing then find out through the voice and calling of God that life really can be something else. Abraham started one race and finished another. Moses started one race and finished another. Ruth started one race and finished another. Esther started one race and finished another. Paul started one race and finished another. God always has another chapter written for you.

So alongside the Sea of Galilee walks this rabbi named Jesus. He's got no business walking alongside the Sea of Galilee because he is living in a world where everybody is pegged. You were who you were. You were Roman or non-Roman. You were Jew or you were Gentile. You were religious or you were nonreligious. You were a Pharisee or you were a Sadducee. You followed the law or you didn't follow the law. You got put into a race, and the world was pretty much committed to keeping you in that race. Jesus the rabbi is supposed to be back at the synagogue, staying religious, but he's out there alongside the sea and he bumps into some fishermen. They've been pegged, too. They are lower-class fishermen who are not religious. They are just trying to make a living, trying to finish the race they started a long time ago. But Jesus walks up to them and says, "Follow me, and I'll make you fish for people. Follow me, and I'll have you finish a race different from the one you started."

"No, no, Jesus. We're fishermen, we're nonreligious, we don't keep the law, we don't race with your type, we smell, we've been pegged. . . ."

"Oh," Jesus says, "you've been pegged. Let me unpeg you. Let me invite you to finish a race different from the one you started. Let me invite you to fish not for fish but for people." When Jesus talks about fishing for people, that's just his code word for "love."

"Let me invite you into a life where your mission is to get people loved. To get people loved."

Jesus walks through Jericho and sees Zacchaeus up in a sycamore tree. He tells Zacchaeus to come down from the tree, and he invites himself over to Zacchaeus's house. Zacchaeus, you see, has been pegged. He's a tax collector, and no people were more pegged than tax collectors. Everybody hated tax collectors; they took your money. But Jesus invites himself over to Zacchaeus's house and says, "Zacchaeus, I want to invite you to finish a race different from the one you started. You've been cheating people out of their money. You've been taking more than what is due. And they got you pegged, Zacchaeus. Now's the time to get unpegged. Now's the time to start giving people money, not taking it. Now's the time to get people loved." So Zacchaeus starts giving his money away. He starts running a different race.

God always has another chapter written for you. You can be unpegged from any peg. There is no point in your life from which you cannot turn and start over.

Did you ever hear of Gordon Wilson? Gordon Wilson was pegged but good. He was Irish and he was a Methodist and he lived in Belfast. He was pegged a Protestant, which made him an enemy of Catholics. Like a good pegged Protestant, Gordon took his twenty-year-old daughter, Marie, to a Protestant celebration outside of Belfast to honor the war dead on Veterans' Day. In the middle of that celebration the IRA set off a bomb that buried Gordon and his daughter under five feet of broken concrete. The two of them survived the initial blast and could hear and see each other under the rubble. Marie grabbed her daddy's hand and said, "Daddy, I love you very much." Those were her last words. She slipped into unconsciousness and died in the hospital a few hours later.

When they pulled the sheet over his precious daughter's face, this good Methodist father had to decide something. He had to decide whether he was going to stay a pegged Protestant. Was he going to just finish the race that he started? In that moment, that Jewish rabbi Jesus came and invited himself into that hospital room and asked him if he wouldn't finish a race different from the one he started.

When he stepped out of the hospital and in front of the microphones—when the world expected to hear anger and insults and names—Gordon Wilson said, "I have lost my daughter, but I bear no grudge. Bitter talk is not going to bring Marie Wilson back to life. I shall pray, tonight and every night, that God will forgive those who killed her." The spirit of Christ, Gordon would tell you, had unpegged him.

From this point forward, Gordon Wilson began running a different race. On that day, this grieving dad began leading a crusade for Protestant-Catholic reconciliation. He wrote a book about his daughter, spoke out against violence, and constantly repeated the phrase, "Love is the bottom line." He met with the IRA, forgave them for what they did, and asked them to lay down their arms. The Republic of Ireland made him a senator. When he died suddenly of a heart attack in 1995, the Irish Republic, Northern Ireland, and Great Britain honored this man who finished a race different from the one he had started.

Flash back to the 1968 Olympics in Mexico City—the Olympic marathon. The gold medalist, silver medalist, and bronze medalist all passed the finish line, and then the rest of the runners came in during the next few minutes. The crowd got up to leave. Little did they know that there was still one more runner out there running the marathon who had yet to enter the stadium. Ten minutes go by. Twenty, thirty . . . forty, fifty . . . finally an hour goes by, and the last-place finisher, John Stephen Akhwari from Tanzania, enters the stadium and runs his final lap, to the applause of just a few. Afterward a reporter asks Akhwari why, when he was so far behind, he didn't just retire from the race. The runner seemed confused by the question and then finally said, "My country did not send me to Mexico City to just start the race. They sent me to finish."

God didn't just send you into this world to start the race. He sent you into the world to finish the race—and not just finish, but finish the race he's got for you. "For we are," writes the author of Hebrews, "surrounded by so great a cloud of witnesses, let us run with perseverance the race that is set before us."

George Ritchie, a psychiatrist who wrote the book *Return from Tomorrow*, tells of interviewing survivors of Nazi concentration camps not long after their liberation, and how he came across a former inmate known as "Wild Bill." He appeared strong and healthy and full of life, so Ritchie assumed that this man had been in the camp only a month or so before its liberation. But then he learned that Wild Bill had been in the camp for six years. Not only that, he had been put on the most difficult of all the work details, averaging fifteen hours a day, seven days a week—all on the same starvation diet as the rest of them. How did he survive so well? Wild Bill told his story:

We lived in the Jewish section of Warsaw, my wife, our two daughters, and our three little boys. When the Germans reached our street they lined everyone up against a wall and opened up with machine guns. I begged to be allowed to die with my family, but because I spoke German they put me in a work group.

I had to decide right there and then whether to let myself hate the soldiers who had done this. It was an easy decision, really. I was a lawyer. In my practice I had seen what hate could do to people's minds and bodies. Hate had just killed the six people who mattered most to me in the world. I decided then that I would spend the rest of my life—whether it was a few days or many years—loving every person I came in contact with.

It's called finishing a different race from the one you started.

I don't know what's going on in your life right now. I don't know how many times you've been around the track. I don't know what race you're running. I don't know what pegs you've been pegged with. But friends, life is not about the race you've started, it's about the race you've finished.

Today the rabbi named Jesus has invited himself into your life, and he wants to know: Is it possible that he could put you on another track? Is it possible that you're being called not to fish for fish but for people? Is it possible for you to be the instrument by which other people will get loved?

UNDER THE CIRCUMSTANCES

Jeremiah 6:16

Two roads diverged in a wood, and I—
I took the one less traveled by,
And that has made all the difference.

MAKE NO MISTAKE; I am a Robert Frost fan. His poetry is apt to have almost as much chance of getting into my sermons as a quote from C. S. Lewis. The preceding lines are likely his most famous and popular. "The road less traveled" is a phrase that is etched into our culture's canon and psyche. "Two roads diverged in a wood, and I— / I took the one less traveled by, / and that has made all the difference." "The road less traveled," of course, is not the title of the poem, though most think it is. The title of the poem is "The Road Not Taken," suggesting, at least in my mind, that life is filled with endless choices—and often choices that at first glance don't seem that much different. The pros and cons are close to the same. The paths before us equally lay "in leaves no steps [have] trodden black."

Which way do I go? Should I go this or that way? I don't know. But whatever choice I make, I am affected equally by the road I've taken and the road I've not taken. One can never go back to an earlier point in life to see what "the road not taken" would have been like. The clock never gets turned back. The choices we make are always enormous, whether we like it or not. Whatever road we take makes all the difference, suggests Mr. Frost.

I think of the movie that came out called *Cast Away*, about a man named Chuck Noland who ends up the sole survivor of a plane crash, stranded on a deserted island thousands of miles away from where anyone would think to search for him. Four years pass before he makes the daring attempt to leave the island and get rescued, which he is—only to find that because everyone had given him up for dead, they had moved on with their lives. His fiancée has married and has kids. The movie ends with Chuck out west in the middle of nowhere, standing at the crossroads of four roads that lead east, west, north, and south; he can choose any one he wishes. Literally his life is starting over, and the road he chooses will make as much difference as the roads he doesn't choose.

You don't have to survive a plane crash, flee a deserted island, and get rescued from sea in order to make a completely new start. You don't need to be a Chuck Noland to get landed at a crossroads. We actually land at a crossroads every day of our lives; that's just the way life is. Just like Dorothy in *The Wizard of Oz*—that Kansas cyclone picks her off the Kansas prairie (at least in her dream) and lands her at the crossroads of her life—at the edge of the yellow brick road and at the path between the witches of the north, the east, and the west. But life is like that, isn't it? It lands us, usually by the choices we've made in the past, at a crossroads every day . . . and we get to choose now, today, which path we are going to take. (I always wondered, by the way, what happened to the witch of the south; I guess the south was witchless.)

Lots of people don't want to see life as a perpetual crossroads. Instead they want to believe that they are on a road they can't leave—that, for whatever reason, they have no choice but to stay on one particular path. Exit ramps, intersections, options, and new directions may abound, but for a thousand different reasons only one path seems apparent. Many people's lives are informed more by the road they've been on than the alternate paths and intersections that lie before them.

Let's say a person gets on some sort of career path. At a young age the person jumps on the road of a certain work life, but then gets some point down the road and says, "Boy, I'd love to do something different, but I am so far down this road that I am afraid to get off. I better stay put."

Some people are on the road of family dysfunction. They stay on this road and keep letting the past dysfunction of their life inform who they are. The dysfunction becomes such a part of their identity that they resist taking the road to something new and healthy.

People on the road of unhealthy habits and addictions face a path that inevitably spirals downward, and person after person on the roadside holds signs that say, "Turn here, turn here!" But a person on the addiction road ignores the signs because the pattern is too comfortable, too much a part of who they are. On the other hand, some addicts refuse to acknowledge how helpless they are.

We are so eager, aren't we, to abdicate our freedom—to assume that we don't have any choices? "I would have done something different," we say, "but I didn't have a choice." Of course that's not true; we always have choices. It's what got Adam and Eve into trouble, when they insisted first to themselves and then to God that they didn't have a choice when it came to the tree of the knowledge of good and evil. God confronted Adam, who said, "The woman gave it to me to eat. I didn't have a choice." God then confronted Eve, and Eve said, "The serpent gave it to me to eat. I didn't have a choice." We are eager to play victim to the circumstances of our lives.

Like the guy who asked his friend how he was. The friend said, "Well, under the circumstances, not so well." And the other guy said, "Well, what are you doing under there then?"

Good question.

I believe Jeremiah points to this question when he speaks to a nation and a people who are on the wrong path. They are on the express train heading in the wrong direction. They are becoming less and less the children of God and more and more the children of a confusing world. They are getting signals from the people around them that they should be one thing or another thing, that they should be concerned about this thing and that thing—and they are losing touch with the heart of God. They are losing their sense of what is important to God. They are interested in the thing that's new, the thing that suggests progress. They are making life more about themselves. They don't care anymore about the people whom God cares about—the poor, the helpless, the lonely, the disenfranchised. The longer down this road they go, the less and less they think they have a choice. "Hey," they said to themselves, "we're living in the sixth century now [sixth century B.C., that is], and we have to keep up with the times!" It doesn't matter how far you go back. The issue of progress was always an issue, but how do you progress and not lose yourself?

So Jeremiah says in 6:16, "Stand at the crossroads!" In other words, as much as you may not think there is another viable path, open your eyes and see that you still have a choice. More than one road lies before you. Acknowledge that with every day comes another crossroads. Today you get to choose what path you're going to take. "Stand at the crossroads and look!" he says. Consider a different way!

Frederick Douglass, the great former slave who advocated for freedom and emancipation said once that he prayed for years and years that God would set him free, but not until his prayers made their way down to his feet and he ran away were his prayers answered. Sometimes we have to stand at the crossroads and see the different paths available to us. Sometimes we have to make a choice.

Jeremiah points to even more than that. "Ask for," he says, "the ancient paths, where the good way lies; and walk in it and find rest for your souls." *The ancient paths.* "Don't ask for the new thing," Jeremiah says. "Don't go chasing after the latest thing to come down the pike." There is a way as old as the hills that has withstood the test of time. It's the old path, because it's the best path, where the good way lies. It's where you find rest for your souls.

Do you hear the echo of Jesus? "Come unto me all you who are weary and heavy laden and I will give you rest. Take my yoke upon you and learn from me, for I am meek and gentle of heart, and you shall find rest for your souls." While we so often choose a path that ends up beating our souls, roughing them up, dampening and breaking them, Jesus and Jeremiah say that on an ancient path the good way lies, where we find rest for our souls.

The path is not always easy nor glamorous. It's not the path that necessarily gets you everything you think you want, but it is the path where the good way lies—the path where you wake up and you say to yourself, "It is well with my soul."

What a wonderful goal in life, to be able to say, "It is well with my soul."

In a wonderful scene in C. S. Lewis's story *Prince Caspian*, the four Pevensie children are trying to make their way through unfamiliar territory. They get to a point where two paths diverge. One road looks a little dangerous and somewhat in the direction away from where they think they need to go. The other road appears to make a little more sense. But as they are trying to decide, Lucy, the youngest child, sees in the distance down the more difficult path the faint image of Aslan the Lion— the Christ figure. It is apparent to her that this is the way for them to go. But the rest of the children don't see the Lion, so they disregard Lucy's eyewitness, vote against her, and choose the seemingly better path. Lucy follows behind. Sure enough, it's a path that only gets them into more trouble.

Finally, when they are in a little over their heads, Aslan appears up close and in person before Lucy again, and this time they talk. Lucy explains to Aslan that though she saw him, and though she knew which path to choose, she didn't really have a choice because the others wanted to go the other way. She felt she "had" to go with them. Aslan looks at her with doubt in his eyes. Lewis tells the rest of the story this way:

> Lucy says to Aslan, "How could I—I couldn't have left the others and come up to you alone, how could I? (Aslan just stares at her.) Don't look at me like that . . . oh well, I suppose I *could*. Yes, and I wouldn't have been alone, I know, not if I was with you. But what would have been the good?"
>
> Aslan said nothing.
>
> "You mean," said Lucy rather faintly, "that it would have turned out all right—somehow? But how? Please, Aslan? Am I not to know?"
>
> "To know what *would* have happened, child?" said Aslan, "No. Nobody is ever told that."
>
> "Oh dear," said Lucy.
>
> "But anyone can find out what *will* happen," said Aslan. "If you go back to the others now, wake them up; and tell them you have seen me again; and that you must all get up at once and follow me—what will happen? There is only way of finding out."

There is only one way of finding out: to choose. But before you can choose, you have to stand at the crossroads. You have to see that every day—no matter who you are, no matter where you are—the crossroads are before you. Stand at the crossroads and look. The road you've been on doesn't have to be the road you stay on. God gives you that choice, and maybe today is the day you make it. And if today is the day to make it, don't dare put it off until tomorrow. For why has the path led you here today, but to give you maybe the chance to choose a different road? The ancient path, the time-tested path—where the good way lies, the path to find rest for our souls.

What better place to end up than the place where we can finally say, "It is well with my soul"?

Is There Fire in Midian?

Exodus 3:1–12

A FEW YEARS ago I had the chance to take a sabbatical leave and do some traveling on my own over in Ireland. During my little jaunt around the Emerald Isle I stumbled upon a place called Glendalough. Glendalough is this incredibly beautiful little valley situated amid the Wicklow Mountains south of Dublin. It is the site of an ancient Celtic Christian community dating back to the sixth century, and it is an area that the Celts call a "thin place." In thin places, one senses that the membrane that lies between heaven and earth is very, very thin. As you dwell in such places, you feel the presence of heaven like in no other place. Glendalough was one such place for me. As I walked through the valley of Glendalough, the membrane was very, very thin.

I spent four days there, and on one of those days I was out for a walk, all alone—likely not a person within a mile of me. As I was enraptured with the beauty of the place, I found myself not only really, really connecting with God, but also really, really missing my family. So I stopped on the trail, reached into my pocket, and pulled out a little black box. I punched a few buttons on this little black box and held it to my ear, and within seconds I was talking with my two most favorite people in the world—Amanda and Brittany, who were half a world away. After we talked I pushed a button on the black box and we were disconnected, and I continued down the path. And then all of a sudden it occurred to me what had just happened. I had just done something that a hundred years ago was beyond the realm of imagination. In a remote Irish valley, with no sign of wires or electricity for that matter, through the help of something way up in the sky that was invisible to me—something I don't even pretend to understand—I was able to be connected to someone halfway around the world. Just as astounding was that as I was placing that call, I was paying no attention to the miracle that was happening. I took it for granted.

Technologically, we are living in the world of miraculous connections. Cell phones are everywhere and the only time we give thought to the miracle of 21st century communication is when we are not able to do it, when we lose our connection. "Can you hear me now?"

While our present technological connectivity is truly amazing, it can blind us from another kind of connection going on in this world, a connection that has been going on for thousands and thousands of years, one that makes cell phones look like tin cans with string. One of the first times we hear of this connection is in this story from Exodus.

The story starts in Egypt, where there is groaning and crying. You remember that the Israelites—that is, the Hebrews—are in Egypt, and they have suffered under the yoke of slavery for a very long time. Their suffering has turned to groaning, and their groaning to crying. The writer of Exodus tells us that their crying has ascended to the heavens. Without the benefit of cell towers, their crying has ascended beyond the clouds into the heavens. And we are told that God—invisible in the heavens, as mysterious to them as a satellite is to me—heard their groaning. God looked upon the Israelites, and he took notice of their slavery, their suffering, their need for deliverance. That is the first half of our story.

The second half of the story takes place in Midian, way over in the Sinai Peninsula, which for ancient civilization was like a trip halfway around the world. In Midian we find Moses trying to mind his own business. He has escaped Egypt and has no desire to go back. He has made his career choice. He is taking care of his father-in-law's sheep, providing for his family, planning for retirement. He is setting aside money in his 401(k). (Or maybe he should be putting it under his mattress.) But then God does something. God starts a fire. This invisible God—high up there in the sky, who has been listening to these cries coming from Egypt—starts a fire in Midian. Moses sees this fire—a burning bush, and not just any burning bush, but a bush that won't stop burning. A fire that won't go out. Moses approaches the burning bush, and out of the fire comes the voice of God calling Moses to go to Egypt where the people are crying.

Do you see what has happened? The people of Israel cry in Egypt, God hears their cry, and God starts a fire in Midian. Long before Verizon, Sprint, and AT&T, God was making connections between people who were far, far away from each other.

For every cry that goes up in Egypt, a fire is started in Midian. We are living in a world that is ruled by an often invisible God, yet this God hears the cries of his people, and when he hears the cries of his people he starts a fire somewhere else. That fire is the voice of God calling his people to respond to the cries he hears throughout the world.

A few years ago a guy came into my office up in New Jersey. Doug had been a business executive his whole life, and when he was able to take early retirement, someone talked him into taking a little trip to Honduras. Doug didn't know much about Honduras, but he thought, *What the heck.* So he went for a week to help on a little mission project. And after spending a week there, and seeing the plight of the citizens of one of the poorest countries in the world, Doug came back unable to get these people out of his mind. Doug walked into my office and said, "We've got to do something! We can't just sit here and not do something! We've got to help these people. I can't live my life and not do anything for these poor people. We have to feed them. We have to clothe them. We have to educate them."

God was starting a fire in Midian. God was starting a fire in a guy from New Jersey, because God had heard the cries of the people in Honduras.

Fast-forward to today, and there is a school there in Honduras, kindergarten through the sixth grade, offered only to the poorest of the poor. One hundred seventy-five kids. They are fed, they are taught, they hear about how God loves them in Jesus Christ. They get medical treatment. They get loved. Doug would tell you that he has very little to do with it, because it all started with a fire—a fire that God started in Midian.

The same thing happened in a town called Sarasota, Florida. A doctor and his wife, Doug and Maxine, saw a fire—a burning bush. Through it they heard the voice of God telling them about the cries coming from Honduras. And they responded, beginning a ministry to people in a town called El Progreso, an eye clinic and later a dental clinic. Tens of thousands, maybe a hundred thousand by now, have been ministered to through that very important mission. People can see again. They can see what is front of them, and they can see what is around them. And maybe they can see who is within them, our Lord and Savior Jesus Christ. God heard the cries in Egypt and he set a fire in Midian.

I have an easy question for you today: Are there still cries coming from Egypt? And what I mean by "Egypt" is the world. Are there cries coming from the world? Is there suffering going on? Are there cries coming from places like Appalachia—people without adequate housing? Are there cries coming from Africa? Are there cries coming from Honduras? Are there cries coming from the Sudan? Are there cries coming from Newtown? Are there cries coming from people you know who are losing their money daily in this crisis? Are there cries coming from inside this church? Are there cries coming from inside you?

The answer, of course, is yes. The world is a tough place. The yoke of living is heavy. Brutal inequities exist. Life hurts. Cries are coming from Egypt.

And with every cry that comes from Egypt, every cry that emanates from this world, every cry that ascends beyond the clouds into the heavens—there is a question as to whether that cry is being heard. Does God hear my cry? Am I making a connection?

Does God hear the people crying in Darfur who are victims of genocide? Does God hear the people crying in Israel and Palestine? Does God hear the people crying in the streets of our inner cities? Does God hear the people crying in cancer wards? Does God hear people crying at your high school? Does God hear people crying in million-dollar McMansions? Does God hear people crying sitting alone at their kitchen table? Does God hear the cries of his people?

The answer is always found in a fire in Midian.

Do you know the story of Flo Wheatley? Flo was just a regular old mom, except that her son was battling cancer. Flo, who lived in Pennsylvania, would have to take the train with her son to New York City to get treatments for his cancer. One afternoon as they left the hospital, her son was very sick. He was vomiting and weak, and she could hardly get him down to the subway station. Then it started to rain. Flo didn't think she could go another step, when all of a sudden she heard a voice behind her say, "You need help, lady?" Behind her was a homeless man wearing ragged jeans, sneakers, and a cutoff army jacket. She was afraid of the guy, so she declined his help. "No," he said, "you need help." And with that he picked up her suitcase and walked with them toward the subway. When they got to the subway and the subway came, the man got on with them. When they got to their stop the man got off with them and hailed a cab for this mom and her sickly son. When the cab came, Flo didn't know what to do to thank this homeless man who had given her so much, so she pressed a five-dollar bill into his hand as she got into the cab. And as she did, she heard the man say, "Please, lady, don't abandon me." And with that the cab sped off.

Flo couldn't stop remembering those words: "Don't abandon me."

During the next two years her son responded to treatment and his cancer went into remission, but Flo didn't stop thinking of those words. Now living in Hop Bottom, Pennsylvania, Flo looked at all the clothes that her children had that they were no longer wearing. And Flo got an idea to take the clothes—sweaters, jeans, coats, whatever—and make a sleeping bag out of them, which she did. And when she was done, her husband drove her into New York City, and they found a man huddled in a doorway in the freezing New York winter, and they gave him the sleeping bag. She went home and made eight more bags that year and delivered them into the city.

Word got out in town what Flo was doing, and Flo spoke about it at a local church. She called what she made Ugly Quilts, and she called her ministry My Brother's Keeper Ugly Quilt Group. Women in the town decided to help. They gathered and made it into a social group. In just a few years the group produced more than five thousand sleeping bags. People from around the area, around the state, even around the country began contacting Flo to find out how to make these sleeping bags. She started sending out instructions. She heard from all over. A missionary in Mexico asked how to make them for the people he served. An army unit in Europe asked how to make them. She learned later that the Flo-designed sleeping bags were being airdropped into Bosnian refugee camps. Hotel chains began donating bedspreads and mattress pads. It is believed that well over one hundred thousand sleeping bags have been made.

When asked if she ever found out who that homeless man was who stopped to help her that fateful afternoon, Flo says yes. She figured out who it was. She says the man was Jesus. That's who stopped her. That's who picked up her suitcase. That's who hailed her a cab. That's who said, "Don't abandon me." She's sure of it. And Jesus started the fire, you know. He started the fire in Flo Wheatley's little Midian. And she saw it, she heard it, and she responded to it, and the cries of the homeless were met.

My question for you is, is there fire in Midian? We know there are cries in Egypt, but is there fire in Midian—that is to say, is there fire right here? Is there a fire burning somewhere around here to which we are drawn and from which we hear the voice of God calling us to respond to somebody's cries? Is there fire in Midian? Is there a fire inside you or around you, one that is beckoning you to respond to somebody's cries?

That question may be one of the most important ones you ever consider. The degree to which you discover the fire in Midian is not only the degree to which people's cries get heard, but it is also the degree by which you will likely discover the real meaning for your life. Moses thought he was settled. Moses was just minding his own business. What would have happened if he hadn't seen the fire? Forty more years of grazing sheep? Forty more years of minding his own business? Forty more years of tending his 401(k)? Thank God he saw the fire. My guess is that if someone had asked Moses if he ever had a thin place, he would have said, "It was when I saw the fire."

Anne Frank said, "Isn't it wonderful that nobody need wait a single moment before changing the world?"

The Theory of Relativity

Matthew 20:1–16

YEARS AGO AN article in the *Philadelphia Inquirer* caught my attention. It had to do with a woman named Catherine Urioste who was driving down the road near Las Vegas, Nevada. It was winter time and the road was icy. All of a sudden she lost control of the car and it skidded off the road and flipped over and plunged upside down into an icy river. Instantly, her upside-down car began to fill with water. With no way to get out, Catherine quickly determined that this might very well be the end. But before she panicked, she remembered seeing on television a certain survival technique. She remembered that somewhere in this car-turned-aquarium there had to be a pocket of air, and that if she was going to survive she had to find that air pocket. So she quickly made her way to the top of the car—which was now the floor of the car—and groped around for that pocket of air she knew was there. She found it by the backseat. This pocket of air was big enough to allow Catherine to keep her head just above the water line, with the water just lapping underneath her chin. She remained there for forty-five minutes, the rest of her body still submerged in freezing waters. It took forty-five minutes before anyone came to Catherine's rescue, but in the meanwhile she just kept her head in that pocket of air, praying and talking to herself and even laughing just to keep herself from losing hope. After her rescue, Catherine said that never before in her life had she understood how precious a thing a small pocket of air could be.

I am not sure the last time I gave thanks to God for a small pocket of air. It is, I suppose, the most frequent gift I receive each day: a small pocket of air that I draw into my lungs, delivering oxygen to my blood and life to my organs. I do not recall the last time I gave thanks for that little moment of inhalation that I call my next breath, but it comes without me noticing it, and my life depends on it.

The reason I don't notice this air is that I have so much more to which I'm paying attention. I would like to say that I am paying attention to the beautiful weather we've been having, or the migrating birds. I'd like to say I am noticing the faithfulness of a friend or the blessing of my family. But I don't particularly pay attention to those things either. What I am paying attention to is my calendar. I am noticing the pile of paper on my desk. The mercurial stock market. I am noticing all those things that you notice. That knocking sound in the car. The crowd that a child is hanging around with. The rumors of more corporate downsizing. The pain in the chest. The burglary down the street. We notice these kinds of things, certainly not our last or next breath—as much as our life might depend upon it.

What does your life depend upon? Is it your next breath or your next appointment? Is it a small pocket of air or the big list of things to do? Is it the expansion of your lungs or the expansion of your holdings?

My father was a twin, the first of the pair to be born. When his brother entered the world the attending physician took one look and deemed him stillborn. They set him aside and attended to my father. By grace an intern walked into the delivery room and noticed the lifeless child and decided to apply some techniques he had recently learned in medical school. Within a few seconds the little lifeless boy drew in his first breath—a breath that led to fifty years of ministry, sixty years of marriage, children, grandchildren, and a lifelong brotherhood with my father. Just one breath. And every breath since is what his life depended on.

What does your life depend upon?

I guess it all depends upon how you define your life. Has your definition of life changed since you first drew in that first small pocket of air? Of course it has. To grow and mature is to see life in a much more complicated way—in relationship to other things and other people. The list of the essentials has changed since we were little babies. We have looked around us and seen what everyone else has or doesn't have, and we have said to ourselves this is what life is supposed to be for me: a little bit more than those people, maybe a little bit less than those people, and just as much as those people. Life sure gets complicated when you are trying to figure it out that way. The longer you live, the more complicated it gets and the more standards you have to fit into the equation. The essentials have changed, from our childhood needs of food and air and parents' hugs to keeping up with the Joneses. And it just keeps getting more and more complicated.

Is it any wonder that, in the list of Ten Commandments, God ends it with the commandment, "You shall not covet. You shall not covet your neighbor's house; you shall not covet your neighbor's wife, or male or female slave, or ox, or donkey, or anything else that belongs to your neighbor"? I used to treat this commandment like we do most things that fall at the end of a list, a little bit like an afterthought. At the top you have the big things: "You shall have no other gods before me. You shall not make a graven image. You shall honor your mother and your father." And even in the middle—"You shall not kill. You shall not steal"—those seem important and basic. But I wonder how much attention gets paid to this last one?

It seems to me that this last commandment—you shall not covet—has so much to do with the rest of the commandments. In fact, imagine if we obeyed the last commandment. Imagine if we did not care two hoots or a holler about what anyone else had. Imagine if we did not desire what was in someone else's possession. Imagine what that might mean for our obedience to the other commandments. If you are not coveting—if you are not wanting what someone else has—then what would be the purpose of stealing? What would be the purpose of killing? If we were not coveting, would we feel less pressure to work on the Sabbath? If we were not coveting, would we be less inclined to chase other gods? Coveting is a core spiritual issue, and it has everything to do with our understanding of what we have been given already. On what does my life really depend?

Our lives seem to depend on the theory of relativity. Not $E = mc^2$, but seeing life in relationship to the people and things around you, and allowing your happiness to be determined by those people and things around you. Never mind those things that my life utterly depends upon. The quality of my life is relative only to the quality of other people's lives. The theory of relativity says that I need only to look at the people of Honduras and say, "Boy, I have a pretty good life." But the theory of relativity says that I need only to look at the bankroll of Bill Gates and say, "Boy, I really don't have much at all." Living our lives by the theory of relativity gets real complicated. The formula of happiness becomes real hard to figure out.

Jesus tells the story about the landowner and the laborers. A landowner goes out and hires laborers to work in his vineyard beginning early in the morning. Then he hires some more to begin a little later, and some more to begin a little later than that. Finally he hires some to begin as late as 5 o'clock. At 6 o'clock, when it comes time to hand out the pay, all of a sudden everyone gets a full day's wage. Something is wrong with that, we say. It goes against every capitalist bone in our bodies. It seems rather unfair, and the reason it seems that way is that we are employing the theory of relativity. We are saying that a person's worth is only relative to the worth of other people. I can only rejoice in what I have received if someone else has received less. I can only be happy with my self-worth if for some reason someone else is worth less. And that is always a dangerous way to live.

But what if we lived into the Tenth Commandment and focused our lives not on what we don't have, but on what we do have?

You may not recall the name of Harold Russell. Harold Russell was twenty-seven years old when he heard the news that Pearl Harbor had been attacked. He instantly joined the army, and during training Harold Russell was handling an explosive device with a defective fuse that went off unexpectedly, resulting in the loss of both hands. A devastating loss. What do you do when you don't have any hands? Russell laid in a military hospital, horrified at his disfigurement and wondering what was left to his life. Then finally came the epiphany, the life-changing thought. He said to himself, or maybe God said it to him, "It is not what you have lost that matters. It is what you have left that matters." Many of you have seen Harold Russell. You probably saw him in the movie *The Best Years of Our Lives* playing a wounded veteran. He won the Academy Award for Best Supporting Actor, and he wasn't even an actor! One of only two nonactors to win an Oscar, and he didn't just win one Oscar for the role, but two! The only person to win two Oscars for the same role. It's not what you've lost that matters, but what you have left.

Do you remember the scene that Luke paints for us in the book of Acts in which Paul and his missionary companion, Silas, have been arrested in Philippi, and Luke tells us that after being arrested they were beaten with rods? Then they were put in jail and had their feet fastened in stocks. Then, Luke says, late into the night, the beaten, shackled men started singing hymns to God.

No, gentlemen, you don't understand. You've lost everything. You're in jail. You are despised. You are broken. You don't even know if you will ever see the light of day again. You can't be singing.

But it's not what you've lost that matters, it's what you have left. And what Paul had left, what Silas had left, was the saving grace of Jesus Christ. The love of God. The breath that filled their lungs. They had everything they needed.

"I have learned," Paul wrote to those Philippian believers, "to be content with whatever I have. I know what it is to have little, and I know what it is to have plenty. In any and all circumstances I have learned the secret of being well-fed and of going hungry, of having plenty and of being in need. I can do all things through Christ who strengthens me."

Do you recall that great first stanza in Robert Frost's poem "A Prayer in Spring"?

Oh, give us pleasure in the flowers today;
And give us not to think so far away
As the uncertain harvest; keep us here
All simply in the springing of the year.

Keep us here! Keep us here! Keep us with what we have now, with our next breath now. With the beating of our hearts now. With the grace and mercy of God now. "Seek first the Kingdom of God and his righteousness," Jesus says, "and all the other things will take care of themselves."

You shall not covet. Easier said than done. I know it is for me. But if I can just imagine that moment when I drew in my first breath, that moment when I was first held to my mother's breast. If I can just imagine the moment when I first realized that God loved me and forgave me. If I can just remember when I met the love of my life. If I can just remember the moment when my child entered the world. If I can recall the last time I had a belly laugh. If I can taste again a drink of cold water on a hot, humid day. If I can think to the out-of-the-blue call I got from a long, lost friend. If I can see the brothers and sisters with whom I share the body of Christ. If I can remember and see all these things and more, then what more could I ever want?

WHEN LIFE PUSHES BACK

Romans 12:9–21

THE SCOTTISH PREACHER James Stewart—one of the great preachers of the modern era—in his sermon "The Gates of Life" said this:

> I think as one grows older, one learns to look at humanity with new eyes of wonder and of reverence: for countless are the hidden heroisms of every day. Doubtless a cynic, looking at human nature, will see only drabness and mediocrity and commonplaceness and irritating stupidity; but the man who sees only that—though he be the cleverest wit imaginable—is proclaiming himself blind and a fool. He is missing everything. He is missing the shining gallantry and fortitude which are everywhere in action. You cannot go through this world with your eyes open, and with some degree of sympathy in your soul, without realizing sooner or later that one of the crowning glories of the world—a thing that might well make the morning stars sing together and the sons of God shout for joy—is the sheer valour with which multitudes of men and women, quite unknown to fame, are carrying themselves in the face of difficulties calculated to break their hearts

One of the great privileges of being a pastor is that by virtue of what you do, you are invited into people's lives at the most important moments: at birth in the maternity ward, at baptism in the chancel, at confirmation when faith is professed, at weddings when love is declared, in sickness when the body begins to give way, and in death when we are ushered into the new life. At each of these moments, you are bound to see a pastor close at hand. What I've learned as a pastor in being invited into these moments is that life is not always easy. Life, in fact, can be very hard. The truth is that from the moment of our very first breath, life has its way of pushing back—throwing at us difficulties calculated to break our hearts.

I saw a bumper sticker that read, "We are born naked, wet, and hungry. Then things get worse."

Bill Bryson—in his charming book *A Walk in the Woods,* in which he chronicles his attempt to hike the entire Appalachian Trail—describes the end of the first day of his pilgrimage, in which he has already managed to lose his partner, Katz, who has fallen far behind. Bryson backtracks to see if he can find him along the trail and writes,

> Finally, I rounded a bend and there he was stumbling towards me, wild-haired and one-gloved and nearer hysteria than I had ever seen a grown person. It was hard to get the full story out of him in a coherent flow, because he was so furious, but I gathered he had thrown many items from his pack over a cliff in a temper. None of the things that were dangling from the outside were there any longer.

And then Bryson writes, "He acted as if he had been deeply betrayed by the trail."

Life can sometimes feel that way—that you have been deeply betrayed by the trail. But that is the truth about life. It has its way of pushing back.

It was that way from the very start, when Adam and Eve enjoyed the splendor of the Garden of Eden, but then life pushed back. The serpent slithered into their company and threw their way the first temptation—the first hard choice—and they failed. Scripture tells us that God shows up in the garden very disappointed with their failure and informs the woman that from now on she will labor in childbirth and the man that he will eat by the sweat of his brow. Life always pushes back.

The question then becomes, what are you going to do about it? How are you going to confront this reality of existence? How are you going to live your days in a life that always pushes back? The question is not whether you will have trouble—Jesus promises us we will, in this life—the question is, how are you going to live into it? How are you going to confront it? How are you going to sail into the wind that wants to push you back?

You know that our biographies are really stories of how we have chosen to face into the pushback of life—what we have done when confronted by the resistance of the world around us. When I read the back covers of the books in the autobiography section of the bookstore, the consistent theme is what they have chosen to do with the unique pushbacks of their life.

Impoverished childhood. Learning disabilities. Abuse. Divorce of parents. Bad health. Physical impairment. War. National crisis. Depression. Alcoholism. Runaway children. Loss of employment.

Every person chooses a way to sail into the headwind. Some work hard and make a lot of money. Some bury their head in the sand. Some sit and stare at the TV. Some eat, drink, and be merry. Some lie, cheat, and steal. Some cloister themselves in spiritual devotion. Some surrender their lives to service. Some sacrifice their lives on fields of battle. But each one of us chooses a way to sail into the headwind, the resistance, the pushback of life.

I think the apostle Paul is dealing with this issue in the last half of Romans 12. Remember his audience: the Roman church. He is writing to the Christian community that gathers at the footsteps of the palaces of the maniacal and messianic Caesars who want nothing more than for these pesky Christians to leave. Soon Nero will literally use the Christians of Rome as human torches to line the streets. This group of people—these Roman Christians—understand something about pushback. And Paul writes to them and wonders with them about how Christians can lean into the resistance. How do we live our lives? How are we to live?

Take no prisoners? Dog eat dog? Every man out for himself? Shoot first, ask questions later? Grab the gusto? Lie, cheat, steal? How do we push back on the pushback?

Paul writes,

> Let love be genuine; hate what is evil, hold fast to what is good; love one another with mutual affection; outdo one another in showing honor. Do not lag in zeal, be ardent in spirit, serve the Lord. Rejoice in hope, be patient in suffering, persevere in prayer. Contribute to the needs of the saints; extend hospitality to strangers. Bless those who persecute you; bless and do not curse them. Rejoice with those who rejoice, weep with those who weep. Live in harmony with one another; do not be haughty, but associate with the lowly; do not

claim to be wiser than you are. Do not repay anyone evil for evil, but
take thought for what is noble in the sight of all. If it is possible, so far
as it depends on you, live peaceably with all.

This is Paul's guide for the trail, his strategy for the resistance, his plan for the pushback, his sails for the headwind.

You won't find any promises in those words. Paul gives no guarantees. He does
not suggest that if we do these things that life will be any easier—or that we will avoid
heartache and pain. He does not guarantee that we will be wildly successful or get
rich quick. What he says is that life pushes back, resistance is strong, and regardless of
how we might think we should meet it, this is how we should live. Love authentically.
Be patient in suffering. Persevere in prayer. Bless those who persecute you. Associate
with the lowly. Live peaceably. Extend hospitality to strangers. These are the core
movements of the Christian life. If you want to know what us Christians do, this is
what we do. Is it practical? No. Will it make you rich? No. Will you make the cover of
People magazine? No. Does it guarantee you a great retirement? No. Nevertheless—
this is how we push back on the pushback.

For you and me, I suppose the critical question is, are we going to buy it? Are
we going to go for this plan? Are we going to embrace this way of life? Or will our
response be, "Whatever"? Will we haughtily view these words as nice sentiment, but
not really grounded in reality?

Swimmer Michael Phelps's performance in the 2008 and 2012 Olympic Games
were historic; Phelps was clearly the headliner of the competition. More Olympic
Gold medals than anyone—truly amazing. But when you stop to think of it, and you
go back to the beginning, swimming—and most sports—is learning how to confront
and push through the resistance. A swimmer confronts the continued resistance of the
water. Michael Phelps at the age of eleven went under the tutelage of a man named
Bob Bowman, who has been his coach since. Phelps has disciplined himself to listen
and to obey the instruction of his coach in confronting the resistance of the water. He
conformed his body, his stroke, and his training to the instruction of the coach. It is
how he pushed back on the pushback.

It's the same in every sport. Teams confront the pushback of the opposing team.
Baseball hitters confront the pushback of the hundred-mile-per-hour fastball. A golfer
confronts the pushback of the course and the weather, and must be disciplined with the

virtually never-perfected fundamentals of stance and stroke. Heather Farr, the great women's golfer of the 1980s, diagnosed with breast cancer—a disease to which she succumbed at the age of twenty-eight—was asked her motto for life. She said, "You play the ball where it lies." You find yourself a good swing coach and create the discipline of stance and stroke and you play the ball where it lies. You face into the resistance.

Who will we choose to coach us into the resistance of life? Whose sails will we set? Whose trail guide will we follow?

On June 8, 1972, I was celebrating my fourteenth birthday. On that very same day as I enjoyed my cake and ice cream, halfway around the world a Vietnamese village was being obliterated by napalm. Men, women and children—most of them badly burned—were left to run for their lives. A photographer captured their desperate flight on film and gave us one of the most indelible images of the war: a naked, screaming nine-year-old girl running for her life. Her name was and is Phan Thi Kim Phuc. She survived. Fourteen months in the hospital. Seventeen operations. Life had pushed back.

Her story since is too long to tell, but in an interview with public radio, she said,

> Although I suffered from pain, itching, and headaches all the time, the long hospital stay made me dream to become a doctor. But my studies were cut short by the local government. They wanted me as a symbol of the state. I could not go to school anymore.
>
> The anger inside me was like a hatred as high as a mountain. I hated my life. I hated all people who were normal because I was not normal. I really wanted to die many times. I spent my daytime in the library to read a lot of religious books to find a purpose for my life. One of the books I read was the Holy Bible. In Christmas 1982 I accepted Jesus Christ as my personal savior. It was an amazing turning point in my life. God helped me to learn to forgive—the most difficult of all lessons. It didn't happen in a day and it wasn't easy. But I finally got it. Forgiveness made me free from hatred. I still have many scars on my body and severe pain most days, but my heart is cleansed.
>
> Napalm is very powerful but faith, forgiveness, and love are much more powerful. We would not have war at all if everyone

could learn how to live with true love, hope, and forgiveness.

If that little girl in the picture can do it, ask yourself, "Can you?"

The answer, of course, is yes. With the power of the Holy Spirit—with our embrace of the word of God, our submission to the wisdom of the apostle—the answer of course is yes.

It's the only way to write the story.

C'EST MOI

Matthew 7:1–5

ASTRONOMER PERCIVAL LOWELL was famous for two things. Through his powerful Clark refractor and with a perceptive eye, Lowell in the early 1900s hypothesized the presence of another planet in our solar system: Planet X, later known as Pluto. Pluto was declassified as a planet in 2006, but Percival Lowell was lauded for his discovery. In fact, Pluto got its name from Percival Lowell, having taken his initials PL as the first letters of its name. (I always thought it was named after the Disney character.)

But Percival Lowell is also famous for his discovery—or supposed discovery—of canals on Mars. Percival Lowell, again through his powerful Clark refractor, could see very distinct lines on Mars that he deduced were canals. From that point, he developed the theory that Mars was likely home to intelligent life that had created the canals, which led to a much wider worldwide fascination with the concept of Martians . . . who might even someday visit us. (Which, most important to me at the time, led to the TV show *My Favorite Martian*.) It took a while before the astronomy community began to doubt Percival Lowell's conjecturing about these lines on Mars, and his findings—and Lowell himself—were pretty soon discredited. No one could quite figure out what Lowell was seeing, or thought he was seeing. The scientific journal *Sky and Telescope* opined that perhaps because of the particular way Lowell adjusted his telescope, he may have been seeing the shadows of the blood vessels in his eyes. He wasn't seeing what was out there; he was seeing what was in here. We don't know if that was actually the case, because we don't have Percival Lowell around anymore. But even if we did, Percival Lowell would have a hard time imagining or distinguishing whether what he saw out there was actually what he was seeing in here.

Imagine that what you are seeing out there is actually what you are seeing in here. Jesus speaks about this spiritual condition in what some would call one of his hard sayings. It may be one of the spiritual life's most difficult challenges: considering that what I am seeing out there is actually what I am seeing in here.

"Judge not," Jesus says, "that you be not judged. . . . Why do you see the speck in your neighbor's eye, but do not notice the log in your own eye?" It's hard to imagine that what I am seeing out there is actually what I am seeing in here.

A Chinese folktale tells of a certain man who lost an axe. Immediately he suspected the boy next door, his neighbor's son. It went beyond suspicion; he was convinced that his neighbor's boy stole the axe. When the boy walked by, the boy looked like someone who had stolen an axe; when the boy spoke, he spoke like a boy who had stolen an axe. Everything the boy did looked like the actions and gestures of a boy who had stolen an axe. Later, when the man was digging a ditch he found the "stolen" axe right where he had left it. To the man's surprise, the next day when he saw his neighbor's son, the behavior of the boy had changed. He no longer looked or acted or spoke like a boy who had stolen an axe. *What a coincidence*, thought the man, *that the boy's behavior changed just at the same time as I stopped suspecting him.*

C. S. Lewis said, "Suspicion often creates what it suspects." Sometimes what we see out there is what we see in here.

The human mind can be a pretty deceitful thing, often believing what it wants to believe—and what it often wants to believe is strangely tipped in our favor.

Example: Get on the scale in your bathroom, and if the number that comes up is a number you like, you feel no need to try it again, do you? If the number that comes up is a number you don't like, chances are good that you will try it once, twice, or three times more to see if by chance the scale made a mistake. We are very gracious when it comes to ourselves.

Psychologists Peter Ditto and David Lopez ran a study with a group of students, asking them to evaluate another student's intelligence. They were given individual pieces of information on note cards about the student, each of which was indicting—not necessarily true, but indicting. The students were instructed that as they went through the cards, they could stop examining as soon as they had reached a firm conclusion on the student's intelligence. Results showed that when the subjects liked the student under evaluation, the students wouldn't stop turning over the cards—hoping that something might come up which would give positive evidence that the student was smart. But if the subject didn't like the student for whatever reason, then it took only a couple of cards to be convinced that the student wasn't really that smart.

What we see out there is often what we see—or want to see—in here.

So, maybe Jesus's statement—"Judge not, that you be not judged"—isn't really that a hard saying for us, because the way the human mind works, few of us may think that we really have a problem with this one. We tend to think more highly of ourselves than we should. A lot of us who hear this teaching of Jesus may say to ourselves, *Yeah, I may judge a little here or a little there, but it's not that much of a problem*. Or, *The judgments I do make are pretty objective and guided by the Bible, so I am pretty safe from what Jesus is talking about*. Seldom do I have people come in and talk to me about the log in their eye. Lots of people talk to me about the specks in everybody else's eyes, but few come in and say to me, "You know, Steve, I need to talk to you about this two-by-four that I've got in my eye." The reason, of course, is that we can't see it. The brain won't let us. The only time we see it is when we are willing to admit that our own issues are worse than those of everyone else we know—and it's creating a problem.

Remember Jesus' discussion about the Pharisee and the Publican. The Pharisee in his prayer goes on and on about all the things that God should be thankful about when it comes to him—how much money he gives, how much fasting he does, and how great that he's not like the tax collector over there. The tax collector says one thing: "Lord, be merciful to me, a sinner."

Paul Tournier, the great twentieth-century Christian psychologist from France, was giving a lecture in the United States about the Christian life. At the end of the lecture a young man stood up and starting railing about how the church's problem is that it is filled with hypocrites, and he went on and on about how so many Christians are hypocrites. But Tournier, who spoke French, did not understand what the young man meant by the word "hypocrite." Someone explained to Tournier that it meant someone who says one thing and does another. And Tournier, realizing finally what the word meant, said, "Ah, c'est moi! C'est moi!" (That's me! That's me!).

"Judge not, that you be not judged." Jesus knows that the more time we spend on the speck, the less time we spend on the log. The more time we make it about someone else's sin, the less time we make it about our own. And God knows I have a lot to work on. How about you? "Lord, be merciful to me, a sinner." *C'est moi! C'est moi!*

But it goes far deeper than that, of course. The truth is that there is probably no more effective way for us to do harm than through judgment. Very little judgment is redemptive outside of God's judgment. You can really hurt a person when you have a log in your eye and you're trying to take out the piece of dust in theirs, especially when you don't think you have a log at all. Imagine sitting in the chair of a blind ophthalmologist. How would that make you feel? There is no better way for us to do harm, Jesus says, than to pass judgment. And if that statement doesn't make you squirm, then you probably can't see the log.

The great French storyteller Guy de Maupassant wrote story called "The Piece of String." It's a story of a French peasant whose name was Hauchecorne. Monsieur Hauchecorne, as the story goes, was walking down the street one day and came upon a piece of string that was lying in the road. Being the frugal man that he was, he could not let an unclaimed piece of string go untouched, so he bent over to pick it up. As he was bending over to pick up this little piece of string, the local saddler, Monsieur Malandain, noticed from his shop a distance away Hauchecorne picking up this object from the ground. There had been bad blood between these two men, so when Hauchecorne noticed that his enemy was observing his miserly act, he quickly shoved the string under his coat and went on his way. Later that day it was reported that a French nobleman had lost his pocketbook containing five hundred francs—and there was a reward for its recovery. Not long after hearing the report, Hauchecorne was stopped by the police, who told him that it had been reported that he had the pocketbook and that a Monsieur Malandain had seen him pick it up off the road; would he please turn it in? Hauchecorne, of course, replied that he had never seen such a pocketbook and that the object he had been seen picking off the road was not a pocketbook, but a piece of string. Not believing him, the police brought him to the town hall, where the mayor ordered him searched. The pocketbook was not found—only the piece of string. With no evidence, the mayor was forced to release him. Of course, by this time the word had gone out into the little village that Monsieur Hauchecorne had been accused of taking the pocketbook. That's all people needed to hear. An accusation was as good as a conviction. Upon his release, Hauchecorne could not speak to a single soul in the town without suspicion being raised as to whether he really stole the pocketbook.

A few days later that pocketbook was found, with the money intact, and Hauchecorne was greatly relieved to think that his name had finally been cleared. But such was not the case. People could not bring themselves to believe that this accused man was not in fact the criminal. The harder he tried to convince people that he had not picked up a pocketbook but a piece of string, the less people believed him. In fact, he became the joke of the town; when people would see him walking by, or sitting in the local tavern, they would beg him to tell the "piece of string" story, just for the amusement of watching what they thought was a guilty man telling a tall tale. Of course, the poor man's soul was crushed, causing him to stay awake at night and lose his appetite. Soon he took ill, and eventually he fell into a delirium. It is said that in his last days all that could be heard from his mouth were the words, "It was only a piece of string, it was only a piece of string."

We know so little of other people's stories, don't we? And judgments produce headlines, but headlines never tell the whole story. Only God can tell the story. And thank God, God has his own plank. His own big piece of wood sitting right in his eye. Two logs actually: the vertical and the horizontal elements of the cross. God looks through these logs, and through them he sees no specks at all.

Why then are we so able to see something different?

God, be merciful to me, a sinner.

C'est moi! C'est moi!

The Cornucopian Life

Genesis 1:26–31

AT THE END of every Super Bowl since 1987—with one exception—the folks at Disney have employed an ingenious advertising campaign. You know what it is. At the end of every Super Bowl, some Disney marketer posing as a beat reporter asks a member of the winning team—usually the quarterback—this question: "You've just won the Super Bowl, what are you going to do now?" And the response is, "I'm going to Disney World."

In other words, you've just reached the pinnacle of your career, what you have been working your whole life for—you have reached the summit. What are you going to say? What are you going to do? Implied is that the first act, the first word, is maybe the most significant.

Look at the very beginning of the Bible—the first chapter of the book of Genesis. Read how God created the heavens and the earth. Day by day God is methodically bringing the universe into form and substance, and he is adding various elements and levels of creation. It all culminates on the sixth and final day, when God creates humankind—man and woman. You are left with no doubt that this man and woman are the pinnacle of God's creation; they are the culmination and the crowning glory of all that he created. He has created them in his image. Nothing else in all creation bears this image. God has just reached the end of the Super Bowl; he has done this amazing act of creation, and he has finished it off with creating living beings that take on his mark. As hearers of this story, we are eager to hear the first words from God's mouth to the pinnacle of his creation. What does he have to say to his image bearers? Of all the things he could say—and God, of course, could say anything—what would be the first thing?

Would he say, "Don't get into trouble"? That would be reasonable.

Would he say, "Be careful out there"? Again, reasonable.

Would he say, "Work hard and save your money"? Also reasonable.

Would he say, "Eat your vegetables"? Maybe not necessary, since that's about all that they had.

Genesis tells us that the first two words from God to his creation—the first words he chose above all the other words—were, "Be fruitful." The first words after the Super Bowl of creation: "Be fruitful." The first order of business: "Be fruitful." God has been fruitful through these days of creation; now it's his creation's turn: "Be fruitful."

Most people reading that passage are tempted to think that God is just saying is to propagate the species: "Go and make babies." And that is certainly part of it.

But we who read the Old Testament through New Testament eyes know that when God says, "Be fruitful," he is saying something a whole lot bigger. From Jesus' ministry and teaching and life, we are left with no doubt that life—your life and my life—is all about fruit bearing. Jesus puts it very directly, "Every tree that does not bear good fruit is cut down and thrown into the fire. You will know them by their fruits." Later he talks about how he—Jesus—is the vine and we are the branches, and that those who abide in Jesus bear much fruit—and because God is so much in the fruit-bearing business Jesus goes on to say, "He removes every branch in me that bears no fruit . . . and . . . every branch that does bear fruit he prunes that it may bear more fruit!" Paul echoes the same thing when he says that we belong to Christ in order that we may bear fruit for God.

Over and over again, Scripture paints this picture of disciples, followers of God, living lives as a fruit-bearing tree that, as the psalmist says, is planted by streams of water and that bears its fruit in its season.

To borrow a different metaphor, God has this vision of our lives as a cornucopia—that horn of plenty in which the fruit is literally spilling out for others to take. For Jesus the abundant life is the cornucopian life—a life that is spilling out fruit.

Think with me about the cornucopian life, life connected to a vine that is bearing fruit. That's the life Paul is describing in Galatians when he talks about the fruit of the Spirit. He's talking about the cornucopian life—life attached to the vine that God is pruning in order to get as much fruit out of it as possible.

Paul says the fruit of the Spirit is love, joy, peace, patience, kindness, generosity, faithfulness, gentleness, and self-control. Sounds like the perfect life. Is this not the picture that we want for ourselves—a life of love, joy, peace, patience, kindness, generosity, faithfulness, gentleness, and self-control?

One of the great promises of Scripture is that as we walk in the Spirit—as we step with the Spirit, claiming our inheritance—the result is the fruit of the Spirit. The fruit of the Spirit are all those things that we, at the end of the day, really want: love, joy, peace, patience, kindness, generosity, faithfulness, gentleness and self-control. Can you get a better list than that?

But Christians make one big mistake when they think about the fruit of the Spirit: We think it is fruit that we get to keep, that it is intended for us, that we are supposed to hold on to it or possess it—that it becomes *my* joy, *my* peace, *my* patience.

"Boy, thank you, God, for how I feel love, for how I feel joy, for how I feel peace. I have the fruit of the Spirit. I am the bushel basket for the fruit of the Spirit."

But no tree bears fruit for itself. No tree grows its fruit and then consumes it. The fruit a tree bears is for someone else.

Remember *The Wizard of Oz* when Dorothy and the Lion and the Scarecrow and the Tin Man come upon the orchard of apple trees? Dorothy goes to pick one, and the tree slaps her hand and asks her what right she has to pick his fruit. Then all of a sudden that whole cast of characters is fighting with the trees over their fruit. When you are a child and watching that, the whole scene is so absurd—because no tree bears fruit for itself.

When Paul talks about the fruit of the Spirit, he talks in terms of not what we receive as much as what others receive when they are in our presence. It's not primarily a question of whether I receive love from God; it's whether those around me receive love from God. It's not whether I receive joy or peace or patience; it's whether those around me receive joy or peace or patience.

The fundamental Christian question is as follows: "As I go about my life, are the chances good that those who come into my orbit—those who gather around my tree—are bound to experience the fruit of the Spirit through me?"

It's quite a question, isn't it? Think about the people in your orbit—the people who intersect with your life on a regular basis—and ask yourself: *Do these people experience love, joy, peace, patience, kindness, generosity, faithfulness, gentleness, and self-control when they are with me? Is this the fruit that emanates from my life? Is it fruit that people can freely pick?* Would the answers be the same if you asked those people in your orbit those questions about you?

Remember when the rich young ruler comes to Jesus and asks Jesus what he needs to do to inherit eternal life? Jesus ends up saying, "Sell everything you have, give it to the poor and come follow me." Rich people like you and me get all nervous that what Jesus is saying is that we should all empty our bank accounts and give it to the poor. And Jesus would say, "Of course! Of course that's what you do. You never hold onto your fruit. It was never intended to land with you. The Spirit is always on his way through you to someone else. In fact it is impossible for a tree to hold onto its fruit. An apple tree cannot hold onto its apples. They must, sooner or later, be picked or fall."

We humans have developed the ability to hold on to so much. We have ways to preserve our fruit—literally. It's what mason jars are for—to hold on to our fruit. It's what freezers are for, to hold on to our fruit. It's also what bank accounts and brokerage accounts are for, and what basements are for—to hold on to our fruit. It's also what spiritual cliques are for.

We all know what happens when you hold on to your fruit too long, it goes bad. I love bananas, but you can't hold on to them too long. You either got to eat them or give them away, but you can't hold on to them.

Do you want to feel alive? Give your fruit away. Do you want to inherit eternal life? Give your fruit away. We accomplish our eternal purpose when someone comes by and plucks fruit from our branches.

We are not rich unless those around us are rich. We are not joyful unless those around us are joyful. We are not peaceful unless those around us are peaceful. We are not gentle unless those around us are gentle. We are not faithful unless those around us are faithful.

In a church I once served, an elder named John was also the president of a small company—a very successful businessman. But John's life had been a walk with the Spirit. Before he left the house to go run his company he would read Scripture, have a dedicated time of prayer, and write some notes of gratitude to people in his life. He walked with the Spirit, and the result was that he bore fruit—a cornucopian life. I knew this because I would find myself wanting to go visit John on a regular basis. About every six weeks I would stop by his house—a very small and modest home for the president of a company (smaller than the house I live in). Every time I was with him, I experienced the fruit of the Spirit. Love, joy, peace, gentleness, self-control . . . you name it. It was there in John's life for the picking. And I always left so encouraged, so much more hopeful, so much more blessed. And so much more aware: the secret to life is not what you hold on to. It's what you give away.

Maybe Shel Silverstein had it right when he wrote that classic children's book *The Giving Tree*. You remember the story—of the tree that once stood tall and full of fruit. The boy that would come and play in its shade and eat of its apples which, as Silverstein writes, made the tree very happy. Over the stages of his life the boy would come and ask various things from the tree. First the boy asks for apples to sell at the market to make money, and the tree gives its apples—and it makes the tree very happy. Then the young man asks the tree for its branches to build a house, and it makes the tree very happy. And then the mature man asks the tree for its trunk to build a boat, and it makes the tree very happy. And then finally the man, now tired and old, returns to the tree, which is now a stump—and all that the old man wants is a place to sit and rest. "'Well,' said the tree, straightening herself up as much as she could, 'Well, an old stump is good for sitting and resting. Come, Boy, sit down. Sit down and rest.' And the boy did." And the book ends with the words:

"And the tree was happy."

It's the cornucopian life. It is the life in the Spirit.

We are not rich unless those around us are rich. We are not joyful unless those around us are joyful. We are not peaceful unless those around us are peaceful. We are not gentle, unless those around us are gentle. We are not faithful unless those around us are faithful.

For before he said anything else, God said, "Be fruitful."

$\mathcal{A}$ $\mathcal{D}$AY IN THE $\mathcal{L}$IFE

Mark 5:21–43

DECADES AGO, TWO psychologists, Daniel Batson and John Darley, conducted a study of students at Princeton Theological Seminary. The purpose of the study was to see how a random group of theology students would do if placed under the precise circumstances of the Good Samaritan story. The study was set up such that the students were asked to give a speech at the adjoining Princeton University campus. Half of the students were asked to speak about their motives for studying theology and the other half were asked to speak on the parable of the Good Samaritan. That was one variable. The other variable was that half the students were told to begin walking over to the university campus and that they had plenty of time to get there to give their speech: the other half were told to begin walking over to the university campus and that they had no time to spare—in fact, they needed to rush. Along the walking route the study directors had placed an actor who feigned some sort of acute trouble—groaning, coughing, slumped over—clearly a person in distress. Who would stop to help the groaning, coughing, slumped-over man?

The results were conclusive: Whether the students would stop and help the hurting man didn't depend on the topic the students were planning to address. Even if they were planning to speak on the Good Samaritan, they were no more likely to stop than the others. Instead, the significant factor on whether they would stop for the hurting man had to do with how much time they thought they had to get to their speaking engagement. Those who were in a hurry were far less likely to stop than those who sensed they had an ample amount of time. The results came as a shock, especially to the seminary students—really, for all us ministry types.

Most of us would like to think that we would be the one to stop and help the hurting man, but the reality is that we tend to make time the judge of what we do and don't do. Time is the great arbiter—so important to many of us that we strap to our wrists a big plastic and metal piece of electronics to know the time *to the second*. We have the sun in the sky, not to mention that there's usually some sort of clock around that tells me the time more specifically. But no, I have to have a digital watch with seconds that tells me precisely how much time I have before what I have to do next. My watch becomes my judge.

Time is of the essence—and one of our culture's great sins is being late.

We are amazed when we read this story about Jesus—the story of the Good Samaritan, but this time it's not just a story; it's an event. And the Samaritan is not a Samaritan; the Samaritan is a Jew, and the Jew is Jesus. And Jesus does not have much time. He is on an important assignment. He is the Son of God—the Word made flesh—and his assignment is to be the instrument of God's salvation in the world. His job is to save the whole world, which takes some time. So we wouldn't be surprised to see Jesus up pretty early in the morning with his calendar open, or his iPhone dinging—trying to chart out the day, scheduling this meeting here and that appointment there. Time is of the essence. It's even worse for him; he's in the first century with no lightbulbs to extend the day. He's got more to do than we do, and less time to do it.

So in the midst of his day, while he is teaching, surrounded by the crowds, the call comes from a man named Jairus that his daughter is sick. "Come, Jesus, and heal her."

What does Jesus say? "Well, okay. Your daughter is sick. But lots of children are sick. First-century Palestine is filled with children who are sick. And I'm teaching here, can't you see? It's a big crowd. They've come to hear me. I can get more done here with more people than with just your one little girl." The story could have gone that way: "I don't have time. I'm thinking economy of scale. I'm trying to save the world."

We would have understood.

But the story goes a different way. Jesus steps away from the crowd and, in a terribly inefficient use of time, makes his way to Jairus's house. Already this day is not going the way he thought it would go. Because he is on his way to Jairus's house he has put himself on a new clock—because Jairus has told him that his little daughter is at the point of death and Jesus must come quick. He has no time to spare. If we were

Jesus's handlers we would get out our GPS and help him find the fastest way to get to this little girl. We would break every speed limit. He's on the clock.

But then there comes this woman, and she has been suffering for a long time. She has some sort of menstrual issue that has rendered her not only weak but perpetually unclean among her own people. Twelve years she's been suffering, and she put it in her mind that she does not want to stop Jesus. She imagines that Jesus must be a very busy person. *He's the Messiah; he's saving the world. Don't stop Jesus. Just try to get close to him to reach out and touch one of the tassels at the end of his robe.* If she can just touch the end of his robe, maybe there would be power just in that—and she might be healed. She gets close enough, falls to her knees, and grabs one of those tassels—and wouldn't you know, the healing power of Jesus comes into her and she is made well! And she did it without stopping Jesus. He doesn't even have to know that she exists.

But what does Jesus do then? He stops. The disciples are tapping their iPhones and looking at him impatiently: "Jesus, you can't be stopping. You have this little girl at the verge of death. You're on the clock." But Jesus stops because he senses that power has flowed from him to another, and a desperate person must be close at hand. He has bumped into this sufferer and must pay attention. So he stops and acknowledges her. He pays attention to her and affirms her faith and completes the healing so that it is not just her body that has been made well but her soul, too.

Sometimes—most of the time— you just have to stop.

Now that's all well and good, but Jesus has just lost time, a terrible thing to lose. And Jairus knows that, in the losing of time, his little daughter has slipped away. "Trouble the master no more, time is up. Go back to what you were doing, Jesus. We have no more time." And Jesus says this to those who feel that they have run out of time, to those who think that it is too late now: "Do not fear, but only believe." "Do not fear that you are out of time, Do not fear that you are too late—just believe." And with that, Jesus continues his journey to the home of Jairus. There he finds outside Jairus's home a crowd of people who know that it is too late. And while Jesus continues on his mission of wellness, they laugh at him because they know it's too late. And aren't they surprised when the little girl walks from the house? All their fear of being late almost kept the Master from entering, from healing, from making her well.

The fear of being late is what kept those seminary students from stopping and helping the hurting man. They feared that they might be late.

Remember the great story that Harry Chapin used to tell in his song "Cats in the Cradle"? It's a song written, actually, by Harry Chapin's wife—a song about a father and son. When the son is born the father has planes to catch and bills to pay and the son learns to walk while the father is away. No time to play catch. No time to be a dad. There were things he was afraid of being late for.

> And the cats in the cradle and the silver spoon,
> Little boy blue and the man in the moon,
> "When you coming home, Dad?"
> "I don't know when—
> But we'll get together then, Son.
> You know we'll have a good time then."

Chapin himself died at the age of thirty-nine—long before his own children grew.

Why are we so afraid of being late?

Remember the story of the little girl walking with her parents, and she is stopping and picking white dandelions and blowing the seeds? Her mother takes her arm and pulls her along saying, "Come now, Susie, we don't have time for that." Susie replies, "What is time for, Mommy?"

We get this idea about time: Time is this sequential course of moments, and time is something we get to manage. Time is something that needs to work in our favor, and f it doesn't work our way, then that makes us late. The Greeks called this view of time *chronos*—the sequential progression of time, the kind of time in which you can be late. But then there was this view of time the Greeks called *kairos*, not *sequential* time but *opportune* time. The right time, the time at hand, God's time. It's the kind of time that doesn't make you late, because you are doing the right thing at the right time. You can never be late when you are doing the right thing at the right time.

I was struck by the story of Paul Goydos, a golfer on the PGA Tour. Goydos has a compelling story to tell about time. When you are a golfer you only have so much time to prove yourself. Usually by the time you get to around fifty, you have exhausted your time to be the best you can be. You have to make the best use of your years. Every year counts, every tournament counts. You can't waste time. But when Paul Goydos saw his family starting to break apart back in 2004—and his daughters needing an extra dose of his time—the golfer stopped golfing. He left the tour and played full-time dad for a year. A year in a golfer's life is an eternity. But he left the *chronos* and entered the *kairos*. Might this have delayed or hurt his chances of becoming a premier golfer? Might this make him late in his plans to be the best? Of course. "Do not fear being late," Jesus says. Take the time at hand. Do the right thing at the right time.

God helps us by breaking our lives into periods of time we recognize as day and night. God makes the human body such that we must sleep or we will die. It is as if to say that we must attend to what is at hand. Focus on each day. Today is all you have. "Do not be anxious about tomorrow," Jesus said. It's all about today and what the day brings.

What will the day bring? Most of what today will bring is what we did not plan. John Lennon, that great theologian, once said, "Life is what happens when you're busy making other plans." Of course, it's true. Within the *chronos* there is *kairos*. And within each day there are people who you bump into and who bump into you. We bump and we bump and we bump, but how little we notice the ones we are bumping into—because we are so busy making other plans. We're so busy trying not to be late.

But Jesus says, "Believe." And when he says, "Believe," he's saying that we can trust him for the moment. We can trust him to do the right thing at the right time. We can trust him to be late. We can trust him to take care of the Samaritan—of the hurting man on the road and the bleeding woman at our feet.

The moment that turned around the life of Francis of Assisi was when he was riding his horse on the Umbrian plain and he came upon a leper. Shocked at what he saw and believing that leprosy was highly contagious, Francis galloped toward his appointed event. But then the voice came: "Stop. Turn around." He did. He returned to the leper, got off his horse, walked up to the man, and kissed his leprous face. It was the right thing to do at the right time. And with that his life changed, because no more would he ever be late. Time now was *kairos*, no longer *chronos*. Life now was lived in days and moments. Life is what happens when we are busy making other plans. May we, in the *kairos*, never fear being late again.

THE GOD OF INTERRUPTIONS

John 21:1–19

IT WAS THE third Saturday of November 1977. Those of you from the Midwest and who have ever lived anywhere close to the states of Michigan and Ohio know what the third Saturday of November means. It is the day of the Michigan–Ohio State game. The day when all the world stops, or at least should stop, while we turn on our TVs and watch the greatest of all college football rivalries; some say it's the greatest of all sports rivalries—a rivalry that has lasted over one hundred years.

So on the third Saturday of November 1977—November 19, to be exact—at the small college I attended in Pennsylvania, I got together with my Ohio State friend (if there can be such a thing as an Ohio State friend), and we found the only TV on campus that worked. We turned on ABC at 12 noon preparing to watch in all its black-and-white glory another epic gridiron battle.

Just before kickoff, all of a sudden but the dreaded words "Special Report" flashed on the screen, and then we heard the even more dreaded words, "We interrupt this program for a Special Report from ABC News." My buddy and I looked at each other in disbelief. How can this be? How can there be a more important news event than the Michigan–Ohio State football game? This is the epicenter of world history!

Instead of the game, we were treated to witness live the arrival of Egyptian President Anwar Sadat in Israel—the first Arab leader to visit Israel in modern history and an epic first step toward establishing a lasting peace between these two historic enemies. Sadat's move was perhaps one of the most courageous steps by a world leader in our lifetime, especially since it ultimately cost Sadat his life. November 19, 1977—the third Saturday of November—was one of the greatest days of Middle East history, perhaps world history.

My friend and I did not view it this way at all. All we saw and all we felt was *interruption*. The resolution of the Israel-Egypt conflict paled in comparison to the resolution of the Michigan–Ohio State conflict. We were angry, frustrated, betrayed, and we could not see what was happening in front of us. We could not see courage. We could not see sacrifice that goes with peacemaking. We could not see someone risking his life for something greater. We could not see history—real history—unfolding in front of us. We could not see redemption. The only thing we could see was *interruption*.

That is the thing about interruption. It comes in banner headlines. It comes blowing a trumpet so loud and off-key that we can't hear anything else. It comes with such annoyance that the only thing we can think of is how annoyed we feel.

I write my sermons on Thursdays. And it has happened more than once that of all the days of the week, Thursday is the day when I turn on my computer and I see that word *Error. Error!* Something is wrong with our computer network; there is an error. I cannot do anything because there is an error. We interrupt Steve's regularly scheduled program—because the computer has an error! *Interruption! Annoyance!* That's all I could see and feel.

Usually an interruption like that doesn't last very long. Usually about an hour, and then I am back to my regularly scheduled program. If you were to ask me what that hour of interruption is about—what redemption I bring to that hour of interruption—I could not tell you. Because that hour of interruption to me is usually not about redemption; it is about *annoyance!* It is about getting angry. It is about frustration. It is about not being a nice person to the people around me. God loses all chance with me in the midst of my interruption.

But I'm not sure that's how it's supposed to go. At least that's not how it was supposed to go with a man called Peter. In the early part of the gospel story we meet Simon Peter along the shore of the Sea of Galilee. He is getting ready to go fishing. Fishing is what his life is about, what he is trained to do. Likely in his family for generations, fishing is in his blood. But then Jesus comes to the shores of Galilee. Jesus calls his name and says, "Follow me." Now the miracle of the story is that Scripture tells us that Simon, along with his brother Andrew, dropped their nets and followed Jesus. Simon didn't necessarily know for what or for how long—he just dropped his net, put his fishing life on hold, and followed Jesus. What follows is Jesus's teaching, Jesus's miracles, Jesus's parables, Jesus's confrontations, Jesus's arrest, Jesus's crucifixion, and Jesus's resurrection—an amazing three years.

But now in our story we find Peter at the end of those three years, and he is back on the shore of the Sea of Galilee (John calls it the Sea of Tiberias). He is there along with some of the other disciples, this group of men who have had together this amazing journey with Jesus—teaching, miracles, parables, confrontations, arrest, crucifixion, resurrection—and now here they are sitting back at the same shore. The question sort of hangs over them: "Now what? Now that we have had these three years of encounter with Jesus, now what? What's next? Where do we go from here?"

Peter's response is, "I am going fishing." Translate those words, and what you hear Peter say is, "I am going back. I am going back to the way it used to be. I am returning to my regularly scheduled program. I am choosing to look at the last three years of my life, my encounter with Jesus, not as a life-altering experience, not as a redirecting, reorienting period of life. No, I am choosing to look at the last three years of my life as an interruption, a blip on the screen of my life. Now it is back to the fish, back to those slimy little things that swim in the sea, back to what I am used to doing. Back to the way life used to be. I am going fishing."

So Peter goes fishing, and the rest of the disciples join him. It doesn't take much to convince them either to return to the old life. They go out into the dark and do some fishing, and John tells us that that night they caught nothing.

John the Gospel writer paints quite a picture here. The disciples go back to the old life, meaning a turn into darkness, a fruitless casting of nets, a dark and empty experience. A return to the old life after you have had an encounter with the risen Christ is bound to mean a dark and empty experience.

But then Jesus appears, and when Jesus appears on the shore, the sky starts to take on some light. When Jesus appears the nets start to take on some fish, and the disciples' faces take on a new expression. They come back to the shore of their original calling and find Jesus there, and they find a sacramental meal there—loaves and fish—and they reconnect with the risen Christ.

Peter has a problem. Well, it's not really a problem—it's a choice. Peter has to decide what the last three years were. Were they really just an interruption, an interim chapter, or just a neat experience? Or were they something else? Were they a calling into a new life, a calling into a life partnership with Jesus, a launch into another world?

It explains why Jesus takes Peter aside and asks him, "Do you love me more than these?" Do you love me more than the fish? Do you love me more than your regularly scheduled program? Do you love me more than the default setting of your life? Three times Jesus asks him. Three times Peter denied him, and now three times Jesus asks him" Do you love me? Do you love me more than these, Peter? Are the last three years something more than an interruption?

Imagine from Peter's perspective: Though he was given the privilege of walking with Jesus for three years—listening to Jesus for three years, witnessing Jesus's power for three years, encountering the risen Jesus after those three years—the gravitational pull to the old life was still so strong that almost without thinking about it, he got pulled there . . . casting nets into the dark.

It makes you wonder about when God tries to interrupt our lives—not for the purpose of being an interruption, but to pull us into a new life. Or maybe when God takes the interruptions of our lives, which perhaps he does not cause, he tries to use them to pull us into a new life.

Has God tried or is he trying to interrupt your life—your regularly scheduled program—in order to pull you into something new? Is God trying to use an interruption in your life as a way of getting your attention so that he can call you into a new path?

When Moses stumbled upon the burning bush, he may have first viewed it as an interruption. But in the interruption Moses heard the voice of God. Pretty soon Moses was on his way to Egypt.

When Paul on his way to Damascus to imprison a few disciples, he was blinded by the light. It may have first come as an interruption. Hysterical blindness, some may have called it. But in the interruption Paul heard the voice of God. Pretty soon Paul was on his way to Jerusalem, not to imprison disciples, but to join them.

When Zacchaeus sitting in the sycamore tree saw Jesus looking at him and then heard Jesus speaking to him and saying, "Zacchaeus, come down out of that tree for I am staying at your house today," it may have come to him as an interruption. But in the interruption Zacchaeus heard the voice of God. Pretty soon Zacchaeus was emptying out the bank account and starting a new life.

A young American girl—a child prodigy—attended Hunter College in New York City at the age of fourteen and shared a prestigious poetry prize at the age of twenty-three with Robert Frost. She reveled in her associations with the Communist Party and took pride in her atheism. When, after all this, the currents of life seemed to start going against her—when her husband's life started falling apart—when the challenges of motherhood got to be too much—and when finally she got a call one afternoon from her husband who said that he felt like he was having a nervous breakdown and that he couldn't stay a second longer at work, but that he felt like he couldn't come home and then hung up . . . then the "interruption" seemed to overwhelm her. She writes,

> For the first time in my life I felt helpless; for the first time my pride was forced to admit that I was not, after all, "the master of my fate" and "the captain of my soul." All my defenses—the walls of arrogance and cocksureness and self-love behind which I had hid from God—went down momentarily. And God came in. . . . [That night] there was a Person with me in the room, directly present to my consciousness—a Person so real that all my previous life was by comparison mere shadow play. And I myself was more alive than I had ever been; it was like waking from sleep. . . . I saw myself as I really was, with dismay and repentance; and, seeing, I changed. . . . I think I must have been the world's most astonished atheist.

In the interruption, Joy Davidman Gresham heard the voice of God and started down a different path, a path that led over the ocean and to meeting a man named C. S. Lewis, and to falling in love for the first time. She married him, this old Oxford don, on her deathbed—and passed away in his loving arms. Amazing what God can do in, and with, the interruption.

What might this mean for your life and mine? We do know for sure that life is filled with moments we did not plan, or ask for, or want. We have learned to expect the unexpected. But is there more to it than that? Is there more to the unexpected than just the interruption? When life throws the curveball, is there something inside the curveball? The voice of God? The chance to hear the voice of God? In those times of grief? In those times of loss or illness? In those times of unemployment or hurt? In those times of divorce or moving away? We want so badly to go back to the old life, to cast our nets in the dark.

But this is not why the resurrected Christ stands at the edge of the shore. No, he stands at the edge of the shore because it is on the edge that he points us to the new life.

"Do you love me," he asks, "more than these?"

THE DIFFERENCE BETWEEN A SAINT AND A SINNER

Exodus 2:11–22

I READ AN article several years ago in the *New York Times* about a man in Mississippi by the name of Brandon who had been convicted of drunk driving and vehicular manslaughter, having caused the death of a four-year-old girl. A tragic story to say the least. Unfortunately, it's a tragic story that gets played out on our streets just about every night. But what caught my eye in this story was the punishment levied against Brandon. Not only had he been sentenced to twenty years in prison, but to make sure that he did not forget what he had done, the judge in the case ordered Brandon to pay a fine to the family of the young girl he had killed. The fine was in the amount of $520. And Brandon was specifically ordered to pay the fine to the family in increments of $1 a week. Brandon was responsible for writing a check for $1 every Friday and sending it to the family as a means by which he would not forget, at least for ten years, that he had caused the death of a little child.

Regardless of what opinion you might have about the severity of this sentence— some of you might think it too severe; others might think it not severe enough—no number of checks and no number of weeks would suffice as a punishment for this kind of crime. When I think of this type of sentence—$1 a week for years and years and years—it makes me wonder what kind of sentences you and I are serving.

To what degree do you and I feel that we have done something in our past for which we are still paying a price today? Hardly a week goes by without someone arriving to talk to me about this or that problem, and after a little discussion we discover that something has gone on in the past for which they feel they are still paying the price.

Maybe a man feels like he never measured up when it came to his father. His dad was a taskmaster, a perfectionist, and he was always getting chastised by his dad over not quite getting it right. Still today, every time he sees his dad, his dad says something or does something to remind him of the person he isn't. Every time he sees his dad he feels like he's writing out another check.

Maybe a woman tried her best at being a mom, but with the way life goes and all the pressures and having to work, she never felt like she was the mom that her kids needed her to be. Every time she's with her kids she keeps chastising herself over the fact that she could have done better. She keeps writing out one of those checks that remind her of the past.

Maybe someone comes in to see me with a failed relationship, or a broken promise, or a failure of resolve—something that they didn't stand up for—and they feel so bad that they didn't stick it out, or at least stick to their convictions. Whether they know it or not—maybe even subconsciously every day—they feel like they are writing out one of those little $1 checks and sending it to somebody. Maybe they are even sending it to God.

We do that a lot. We send these little $1 checks to God, and we say, "You know, God, I know that you say that you are a God of forgiveness—but just in case you're not, here's my $1 check to make sure we're covered for all the bad things I've done."

How about you? Is there anything you're still paying for? Any sentences you're still serving?

I think it's an amazing thing that one of the great prophets of the Old Testament, one of the great leaders of Israel, one of the models of Scripture, did some hard time: Moses. It's not uncommon for the heroes of Scripture. Joseph did time. Daniel did time. Jesus did time. Paul, Peter, John the Baptist . . . So here we are with Moses, doing time. Self-imposed time, really. He was a fugitive; he committed murder, and when the word starting getting out, that's when Moses took off. Fled for Midian. Never ended up behind bars; his sentence was exile, from his people and from his family.

It's not the story we often hear about Moses. Instead we hear about the bulrushes, the Passover, the parting of the Red Sea, the Ten Commandments—but we don't often hear about Moses on the lam. But there he is. Can you imagine him at whatever age he is, making his run for the border, leaving everything behind and saying to himself, *This is it. My life is over. I have become an alien, a fugitive, a refugee. I am going to spend the rest of my life making out those $1 checks.*

Moses, like all of us, had a past. He was running away from something. But that's really not the issue, is it? The issue is not whether Moses had a past. The issue is, does Moses have a future?

We who know the story know that Moses indeed has a future. But how was he to know it when he was fleeing for his life? This is not the way you prepare the man who is going to be one of the greatest leaders in the history of human kind. Hello? Can we see some SAT scores, please? Can we see his high school transcript? Can we see what college he went to? A resume? All we got is an illegal immigrant!

Why does the Exodus writer feel obliged to tell us about Moses's past? Why didn't he just start with the burning bush? Why did he have to include all this seedy stuff? It never gets mentioned again. No one talks about how Moses was a murderer. Pharaoh doesn't bring it up. The Egyptians don't bring it up. The Israelites don't bring it up. Why does the Exodus storyteller spill the beans?

Could it be that the reason we hear about Moses's past is that we all have a past? Could this dear old saint—and you don't get more saintly than Moses—have had just as much of a past as you and I? Could it really be true what Oscar Wilde once wrote, that the difference between a saint and a sinner was that every saint has a past, and every sinner has a future?

The Bible is littered with people with baggage. Jacob had a past; he was a lie and a cheat. Joseph had a past, sold into slavery by his own brothers. David had a past as a fugitive and an adulterer. Peter: faithless, cowardly, denier. Paul: murderer. The woman at the well had a past. The woman caught in adultery had a past. Mary Magdalene had a past. And every one of these who had a past, the Bible says, also had a future.

Do you know that about yourself? The God who knows your past is the God who has great plans for your future. God wants to take you into his future by prying your fingers off your past. He wants to cancel the $1 checks. He wants to erase the old tapes. He wants to insert some permanent amnesia. When we say that God has a future for us, we are not saying that God just has more things for us to do, more jobs, more tasks, more chores, more assignments, more thankless labor. No, when Scripture says that God has a future for us, he's talking about a new creation. He's talking about going to Midian and starting all over. He's not talking about an old dog doing new tricks. He's talking about a whole new dog!

The story—some say it's true—is told of the missionary priest in the Philippines who throughout his ministry had carried the burden of a secret sin he had committed in his youth. He had never spoken a word of it to anyone, but the guilt continued to crush him. In his parish was a woman who deeply loved God and who claimed to have visions in which she spoke with Christ and Christ with her. The priest was somewhat skeptical. One day he said to the woman, "Okay, if you and Jesus have this conversation back and forth, the next time you speak to each other, ask him what secret sin your priest committed when he was a young man." The woman agreed.

A few days later the priest asked the woman, "Well, did Christ visit you in your dreams?"

"Yes, he did," she replied.

"And did you ask him what sin I committed while in seminary?"

"Yes."

"Well, what did he say?"

"He said, 'I don't remember.'"

Every saint has a past, and every sinner has a future. Can you imagine that you have a clean slate? Can you see yourself getting a do-over? But maybe just as important as that, can you imagine that everyone in your life gets a clean slate with God? That everyone in your life gets a do-over? Can you imagine that that's what this body is all about? We are the body of people who are in the business of do-overs. If you want a second chance, find yourself a church. If you want to stop writing $1 checks, come to the communion table. If you want a clean slate, if you're a sinner and you want a future, if you think you blew it but you want to be a saint, come on in. Can you envision this?

Did you read about the Mennonite Church in Landisville, Pennsylvania, in which a fourteen-year-old son of the church murdered his parents and sister one Sunday afternoon? The tragedy obviously shook that body of people. Devastated the community. What's the church to do? They established a legal support committee to provide for the boy's needs so his surviving brother and sister wouldn't have to. The church founded a "seventy times seven" fund to collect money to cover the boy's expenses. They studied grief and forgiveness in sermons and Bible studies. The held a service of lament for those they lost and a service of forgiveness for the one who remained.

Why? Why, for God's sake, why would they do this? Because God doesn't give up on anybody, and that means *anybody*. Every saint has a past, and every sinner has a future.

In a previous church I served we had appear in our pews one Sunday morning a man who didn't quite fit the prototypical Presbyterian profile. Bob was a little disheveled, a little smelly, a little inarticulate. Didn't seem to have a full deck upstairs. Bob kept coming every Sunday. I went to visit him in his apartment, which was even smellier and more disheveled than he was. I invited him to join the church if God was so leading him. So Bob came to the new members class—a series of classes. He was there at every one of them. Then it came time for Bob to meet the session. A few minutes before the session meeting Bob came to my office and told me he couldn't join the church.

"Why not, Bob?" I asked.

"I don't think I'm allowed."

"Why not?"

"Because I did time."

"You did time, did you? Where did you do time, Bob?"

"The Northeast Center for the Criminally Insane."

"Oh. And what did you do time for?"

"I murdered my wife."

"Oh."

Bob went on to tell me the story. It was true; he was criminally insane at the time.

"So you see," he said, "that's why I can't join the church."

I said, "Bob, do you believe Jesus loves you?"

"Yes."

"Do you believe Jesus died for your sins?"

"Yes."

"Do you believe that Jesus still has a plan for your life?"

"Yes."

I said, "Well, then, welcome into the kingdom."

A couple of years later, it was my last Sunday at that church. Bob came to my office, and he had a painting—a beautiful painting of a church. Beneath it was a caption: "A Future with Faith." I said, "Where did you get the beautiful painting, Bob?"

He said, "I painted it. I painted it the year you were born. I painted it when I was in the Northeast Center for the Criminally Insane. I want you to have it. Because it's true," he said. "What I wrote back then, it's true. I do have a future with faith."

Every saint has a past, and every sinner has a future.

WELCOME TO MY LIFE

Luke 16:19–31

"Something there is that doesn't love a wall." Many of you know those words as the first line of Robert Frost's great poem "Mending Wall." The poem tells the story of two neighbors who meet every spring at the wall that divides their property. It is a stone wall that every winter loses some of its stones, which fall to one side or the other, creating gaps. One spring day each year the two neighbors meet to put the stones back in place and to keep the wall erect and complete. As they go about this annual ritual of mending the wall, the narrator wonders with his neighbor if there is any point to reconstructing the wall. The wall was originally there to keep the cattle from roaming from one property to the next, but neither has cattle anymore. Now all they have is orchards, and there is no risk of the fruit wandering from one field to the next. Why do they need to keep rebuilding this wall? The neighbor's response is the now timeless phrase, "Good fences make good neighbors." The narrator states,

> Before I built a wall I'd ask to know
> What I was walling in or walling out,
> And to whom I was like to give offense.
> Something there is that doesn't love a wall,
> That wants it down. . . .

I would guess that most of us find some sense in the insistent neighbor's words, the one who wants to keep that wall between properties up and in good shape: "Good fences make good neighbors." In the affairs of life we have seen the wisdom in keeping walls erect between neighbors—to make it clear whose land is whose land, whose life is whose life, whose turf is whose turf. Civil courts are filled with folks who have not managed to draw good enough distinctions. "Good fences make good neighbors."

I suppose this principle, this adage, grows to include the idea that we should mind our own business. Over time a person comes to learn that one of the best ways not to get into any trouble is to not get involved. Mind your own business. Keep out of other people's fields. If they need your help, they will ask for your help. But until then, mind your own business. Keep the fence high. Don't get involved.

The inference is that the best way to be a neighbor is not to be a neighbor. The best way to stay friends is to not really be friends. The best way to share a boundary is to make the best wall you can make. We stick to ourselves. We stick to our families. We stick to our country. We stick to our race. We stick to our culture. "Good fences make good neighbors."

Frost's line certainly would have been the predominant view in first-century Palestine. The divide between Israel and her "neighbors" was significant. Not so much the physical divide—Israel had been swallowed by the Roman Empire and now the boundaries were rather blurred—but the racial-ethnic-gender divide was huge. In the first century there were the Jews and everybody else. There were men and there were women. There were adherents to the law and there were the unclean and the unrighteous. The fences that ran between these "neighbors" were as tall as a skyscraper, and God forbid that anyone should try to pass.

Yet the New Testament teaches that God does not forbid such passage. God in the flesh in Jesus Christ walks throughout Palestine, and with every fence he meets he finds a way through. The fence between the righteous and the unrighteous—he finds a way through and ends up eating with tax collectors and sinners. The fence between the Jews and the Gentiles—he finds a way through when he heals the centurion's daughter. The fence between the Jews and the Samaritans—he finds a way through by telling the story of the Good Samaritan. The fence between men and women—he finds a way through by engaging the woman at the well in a conversation. The fence between the clean and the unclean—he finds a way though by reaching out and touching the ten lepers. The fence between the rich and the poor—he breaks through when he tells the rich man to sell everything he has and give the money to the poor. Nobody, it seems, is off limits when it comes to Jesus. Good fences, in his book, make bad neighbors.

You wonder if that isn't the point when Jesus tells the story about the rich man and Lazarus. "There was a rich man who was dressed in purple and fine linen and who feasted sumptuously every day. And at his gate [or shall we say, his fence] lay a poor man named Lazarus, covered with sores, who longed to satisfy his hunger with what fell from the rich man's table." That's the way Jesus lays out the scene. At the center of the scene is a gate, a fence. Now a lot can be said about the disparity between the rich man's wealth and the poor man's poverty—certainly an issue to reckon with—the even deeper issue in the story is the gate. Something about the rich man wants to keep the poor man out of his life. It's what gates and fences are for; good gates and good fences keep people out, or at least keep out the people you want out.

But then comes the twist to the story. Not only does the rich man get what he wants in this life, he gets what he wants in the life after as well. In this life he gets his gate, he gets his separation, and in the next life he gets the same thing. He gets his chasm. He gets this canyon between himself and Lazarus. The rich man has managed to keep Lazarus out of his life forever. But the problem is now the rich man's self-imposed isolation, which turns out to be hell. Lazarus has gone to the bosom of Abraham, and the rich man has gone to where he can be by himself. Jesus calls it Hades—the place of the dead. That's what death is, Jesus says. That's what hell is, the desire to be separated, the desire to be isolated, the desire to keep people away.

In C. S. Lewis's book *The Great Divorce*, he tells of several citizens of hell who are given the chance to accept the invitation into heaven. They make their way as a group up to the realm of heaven. Just at the edge they are invited in, but nearly all of them refuse. They refuse to go into heaven because they want heaven on their own terms. One man in particular has spent his whole life keeping himself away from another man who had committed an offense against him. When he learns that this man who has offended him is now in heaven, he refuses to go in with him. "I'd rather be damned," the man says, "than go along with you." The man is granted his wish. He's damned.

So the rich man who wanted to separate himself from the poor man gets what he wants forever. From Jesus's view, the point is that to live in separation, to live in isolation, to live behind the gates and fences is to live outside the kingdom of God. The kingdom of God is a kingdom of hospitality, a kingdom that says, "Welcome to my life! Welcome to God's life in me. Welcome to whatever I have to offer you." The kingdom of God doesn't appear to have any fences.

That may come as unpleasant news. We manage over the years to erect a whole lot of fences and gates, don't we? In Florida we have tons of gates. We have gated communities. I live in one. We have fences around our property—ostensibly, maybe, to keep the dog in, but maybe to keep out others—and large bushes so that no one can see in. Those may not even be the biggest fences we build. Our biggest fences may come in the simple patterns by which we live. Do I keep certain people out of my life? People of a different culture or color? People of a different orientation or party? People of a different socioeconomic class or religion? People of a different generation? I may have placed around myself an invisible fence. a force field, a sign that says, "You are not welcome into my life."

I grew up in a town that had a huge fence that went around it and a locked gate at every road into town. You couldn't see these things. There were no bricks or pickets or iron rods. People of color were presumed not welcome. So when the first African American family moved into town, or tried to move into town, every attempt was made to stop it. And when their junior-high-school-age daughter started school they wouldn't give her a locker for her coat and books. She had to keep them in the office. One day, a seventh-grade girl walked into the office and said, "I want her as my locker partner." The seventh-grade girl took down the fence and said, "Welcome to my life."

It is, of course, why God in Christ appears in the flesh and walks the dusty trails of Palestine. Over and over God is saying through Jesus, "Welcome to my life." The sinners and the tax collectors. The Jews and the Gentiles. The rich and the poor. The righteous and the unrighteous. "Welcome," God says, "to my life."

Just before I started my senior year in high school, my father, a Presbyterian pastor, said that a young woman whom he had been counseling was going to move in with us. She had a pretty tough home life and was suffering from a severe eating disorder, and she needed a little stability, so she was going spend a few months with us. I was the youngest of four and the last left at home. This senior year was supposed to be about me. In fact, as a seventeen-year-old, the *world* was supposed to be about me. I did not need any interference from an outsider. My father, unfortunately, had not gotten that memo. She was moving in, and I was to "deal with it." She penetrated the gates of the McConnell home and moved into our lives. And it was bumpy and confusing and fraught with ups and downs. There were tears and hurts and laughs and lessons, and after all was said and done, things started getting better for her. She reconnected with her family. And I got a senior-year education that left me a different person, I think—all because someone thought to say, "Welcome to my life."

What would it look like for us to live in such a way that broadcasts, "Welcome to my life"? No more gates. No more fences. No more force fields. Just hospitality. Just an invitation to step into my life.

The story is told about a woman who was nearing death and the pastor came to visit. They talked awhile about the woman's life and her impending death. The pastor, thinking to comfort the woman, said, "Well, Sally, just think. Everyone you love will be in heaven."

"No, pastor," Sally corrected him, "it's not that everyone I love will be in heaven. It's that everyone in heaven I will love."

"Something there is that doesn't love a wall."

RUNNING ON EMPTY

Matthew 25:1–13

MY CONFESSION: I have run out of gas four times. I don't suppose that comes anywhere close to being a record—and if it is anywhere close, I don't think I want it recorded. One of those times I was on my way to a job interview. If you want a sinking feeling, be on your way to a job interview and listen to the engine sputter and see the needle rest on E. By God's grace I managed to coast down a hill and into a gas station. I made it on time. Two of the other times I ran out of gas in the very same place. That might be a record—in the same place and in front of the same house. If you think it is embarrassing to knock on someone's door and ask to make a call because you ran out of gas—this was before cell phones—try doing it a second time. And one of my elders, no less!

Running out of gas is easier than you might think. All you have to be is a little distracted, a little preoccupied, a little bit in a hurry, a little absent-minded—and before you know it the tank is empty and the engine is choking and you are mildly panicking.

The truth of the matter is that many, many people are running out of gas. They are going and going and going—and unlike the Energizer bunny, they do not have a battery on their back. They have tanks in need of refilling, but they are going and they are going and they are going, and they are not stopping.

Pastors will tell you that we answer a lot of calls from people who have broken down. They have been running on empty for too long. Nothing is left in the tank. Emotionally, relationally, spiritually they are broken down. Their marriages are broken down. They forgot to stop for gas along the way—and they are empty, and they do not know what to do.

A lot of us live lives in which we don't want to stop. Some of you are thinking about tomorrow: Monday. The alarm clock will go off—and it is off to the races. Exercise. Work. School. Practice after school. Chauffeuring the kids from school to lessons to practice to dinner to homework. Church meetings. You name it. No time to stop. Even when we stop, we really don't stop.

They did a study up at the National Zoo in Washington, DC, a few years ago in which they discovered that the average time visitors spent looking at any individual exhibit was seven seconds. Seven seconds. We can't stop even when we are stopping. N wonder we are running out of gas.

For most of what I have been talking about, the answers lie in making the necessary adjustments to your lifestyle: erecting healthier boundaries, paring down the list of things you are doing, accepting a simple way of life, learning how to say no, getting a little counseling for your marriage. These things help you refill your tank.

But Jesus talks about another kind of refill in Matthew 25: the return of Christ, the second coming, the day of judgment. Presbyterians don't generally like to talk about these ideas. The Bible talks a lot about it, but we sort of hold this whole idea of the world ending a little bit at arm's length. We know it's there and we know Jesus talked about it, but we would kind of like not to have to deal with it. It conjures up images of some long-bearded man walking around with a sandwich board that proclaims the world is going to end. But that's just not something we want to entertain. We're too busy doing other things to have time to deal with it.

But Jesus wants to deal with it, and in Matthew 25 he talks about it through the story of the arriving bridegroom. Apparently the custom within first-century Judaism was that when a wedding was about to start, the groom would make a ceremonial approach to the place of marriage and the bridesmaids would form a processional with their lamps of oil and light. In this story the bridegroom is delayed. The bridesmaids keep their lamps lit awaiting his arrival, but his arrival is taking longer than expected, and now the issue becomes one of oil supply. The bridesmaids were having a first-century Middle East oil crisis. Five of the bridesmaids are wise, because they have brought an extra supply. Five are foolish, because they haven't. When the groom finally arrives, five are full and ready, lamps ablaze—and five are empty. Their light has gone out. Five get into the party and five don't.

Jesus raises an interesting point: Just because you're a bridesmaid doesn't mean you're getting into the party. The groom is talking to the wedding party, and he says that just because you're in the wedding party doesn't mean you get to go to the wedding. It's not just about being a bridesmaid; it's about doing what a bridesmaid does. Jesus's message to the church is that a time for judgment will come, a time when the groom returns, and what will be looked for is whether there's oil and fire.

Jesus raises the stakes for us disciples. It's not just about being a disciple. It's about what being a disciple calls you to do. We replenish the lamps of our faith by what we do, by how we live, by our obedience to Christ, by our pursuit of God's call, by our witness in the world, and by the stewarding of our resources. This is how the light keeps going.

This great heresy in the church holds that once you get your lamp of oil and fire, that's all you need to do, like it's some kind of eternal flame that doesn't need more oil. Oh no, Jesus says; you must bring your extra flask, which is your day-to-day living within the call of God. History is filled with disciples holding empty lamps, and somehow they think the lamp is all they need. No, says Jesus. You need the oil and the fire, too.

Our lives are a preparation for the coming of the groom. It is what I love about Jesus; he raises the stakes on our lives. We receive so many messages in this world that are intended to lower the stakes on our lives. Economists say we're just consumers. Politicians view us as voters. Biologists claim we're just containers of protoplasm. Sociologists claim we're social agents struggling to live in different levels of society. It's all a process of reducing us into manageable constructs of understanding. But Jesus doesn't reduce us; he raises us. He says that our lives are a preparation for the coming of the groom. And the groom, when he comes, invites us—if we are prepared—into the great feast, the grand party, the big dance.

It all goes back to the oil and the fire—what we are doing in the joyful preparation for the coming of the groom.

A while back I received a newsletter from a rescue mission that we supported— a Salvation Army–type mission. An article reported on how they had sent out a financial appeal for Christmas to their mailing list, and mistakenly they had sent one to a seven-year-old girl named Jennifer. Thank God they did. Jennifer took the appeal seriously. "Mom and Dad," she said, "these people need help." So she figured out that if she saved her allowance for a few weeks she could get to the "minimum" gift— twenty-five dollars. So she did. And all along she prayed for the men she was going to help. And when she got to that twenty-five dollars, she was so happy to be able to send it in along with her note about praying and hoping the gift would help. The mission wrote back a nice note to Jennifer telling her how much her gift meant. It seemed so much fun that Jennifer hated for others not to be included, so she started a matching gifts program. Whatever she saved from her allowance, the adults in her life were challenged to give the same. She wanted them to feel the same joy she did. When asked about this whole thing, Jennifer responded, "What's the big deal? I'm just helping the Lord!"

Now some would call that cute, but I would call it oil and fire. The joyful preparation for the coming of the groom.

So much of our lives—their fullness or emptiness—has to do with what we think our lives are all about. If your life is all about is getting your kid into college, then that is how full your life will get. If your life is all about the latest report from Dow Jones, that's how full your life will get. If your life is all about your last round on the golf course, that's how full your life will get. If your life is all about your most recent purchase for your wardrobe or house, then that's how full your life will get. And none of these things have anything to do with oil and fire.

But if your life is about the joyful preparation for the coming of the groom, then it is all about the oil, all about the fire, and all about the joy of being invited into the party.

Maybe you've heard the story about the father on his way to church with his daughter. He decided he would try a little stewardship experiment. He gave his daughter a dime and a silver dollar, and he told her that she could decide to put in the basket whichever one she wanted. The offering came around, and the father watched as the little girl put the dime in the basket. When they were returning home he told his daughter that he saw that she had given the dime.

"How did you make that choice?" the father asked.

"Oh," said the girl, "I know the Bible talks about how the Lord loves a cheerful giver, and I figured that I would be a lot more cheerful if I gave the dime instead of the dollar."

If we were brutally honest with ourselves, we probably all think the same thing. Perhaps we have been convinced that our lives are less than what they really are, that the measure of our lives is somehow related to the number on our financial statement, the institution name on our diploma, the trophy in our cabinet, or the address of our house. None of these have the oil. None have the fire.

So much in this life distracts us, pulling us one way or the other, telling us that our lives are less than what they are. Before we know it, the needle is on E. But joyfully preparing for the coming of the Lord is all about the oil and the fire.

Maybe this is what the *New York Times* was pointing to when they published the obituary of Helen Bunce. Helen had died at the age of eighty-six in a nursing home in Watertown, New York. She hadn't made much money, didn't graduate from any college of note, held no position except to be a wife and mother and grandmother and great-grandmother—but none of these things get your obituary published in the *New York Times*. So why Helen Bunce? As it turned out, right before her death it was discovered that she was the Mitten Lady. For forty-seven years the Mitten Lady had, day in and day out, knitted mittens and caps for children whose parents could not afford winter wear. Somewhere close to five thousand mittens and caps the Mitten Lady knitted, and with each one she included a note: "God loves you and so do I. The Mitten Lady." For forty-seven years the Mitten Lady knitted and would secretly send the mittens to her church, which would distribute them to people in need. For forty-seven years no one knew that it was Helen Bunce. But finally her cover was blown when they found her in her room at the nursing home knitting her mittens lying on her back—because she could no longer sit. They brought her finally to her church, where, she said, she had to endure the five-minute ovation.

"It's not for this applause that I do this," Helen said. "It's for the children and for the Lord."

It's all about the oil, you see. And it's all about the fire. The joyful preparation for the coming of the groom.

⟨T⟩HE ⟨S⟩TART OF ⟨S⟩OMETHING ⟨B⟩IG

Matthew 13:1–9

No MATTER HOW big, everything started from something small.

In James Michener's classic historical novel *Hawaii*, the great storyteller begins his tale at the beginning. The very beginning. He imagines the central Pacific without the islands of Hawaii and postulates the tens of millions of years it took for these small masses of land to emerge—the volcanic activity of the ocean floor, the emerging mountains of molten rock, the descending glaciers of the ice age . . . and finally the islands that emerged and remained above the oceanic waters. Michener then imagines how long it must have been—tens of thousands of years—before anything resembling life began to form on those volcanic islands. And he imagines the day when upon this barren rock lands a bird, some tropical bird which with the help of the Pacific wind currents has drifted to these islands. From some previous vegetative feast this bird happens to bear inside a seed or two left over from the digestion of some exotic plant. The seeds are deposited, and one manages to trickle down into some crevice where there is just enough soil into which it embeds. The rain and the sun do their part; the seed germinates. A plant grows. Seeds form at the ends of stalks, and the wind scatters the seed to other crevices. More germination. And what results over the next series of millennia are what we now know as the islands of Hawaii. I've never been, but they tell me it's beautiful. A paradise, they say. A place where close to 7 million tourists make restorative pilgrimage every year . . . and all from a tiny seed.

No matter how big, everything started from something small.

Subtract from your age the amount of years and days you've lived plus around nine months and what you have is the time when inside a woman's body there floated about a zygote on its way to be imbedded within her uterine wall—the implanting of a seed. (That's how my mom explained it anyway. She called it a seed; she said I started as a seed. That sounds a lot better than zygote.) It began for all of us with a seed invisible to the naked eye—and the spirit of God—resulting in the likes of me and you. It all began with a seed—the start of something big.

No matter how big, everything started from something small, something very small. That's the way it works.

So it makes all the sense in the world when Jesus gets talking about the kingdom of God—the vast, overarching kingdom of God, the all-encompassing kingdom of God. He tells us that the kingdom of God in you and in me—something that gets started with something very, very small. It's something that gets started with a seed. It is the way life works. No matter how big, everything started from something small.

"The kingdom of God is like a mustard seed, which, when sown upon the ground, is the smallest of all the seeds on earth; yet when it is sown it grows up and becomes the greatest of all the shrubs, and puts forth large branches, so that the birds of the air can make nests in its shade."

The truth is that if you are reading this, it's likely because somewhere along the way—in some pocket of tilled and fertile soil within you—the seed of the kingdom fell and took root. It germinated. It began to grow. And it has resulted in your curiosity about these words. Hopefully, it has resulted in much more than that, but it has at least resulted in you opening this book. Or maybe you are reading this book in order that the seed of the kingdom might fall upon you and embed and take root and grow. The winds of the Spirit have led you here, and the seed of the kingdom is being scattered upon you. Regardless, the truth of our lives is that we are beds of soil where small seeds are planted, and those seeds have potential to become something big.

As with all things in this broken world, this truth can be good news and bad news.

Our souls—like any bed of soil—can grow good and bad.

Those of us who have any type of plant bed in and around our houses know this. The plant bed around my house has the potential of producing some amazingly beautiful flora. Lovely shrubs and plants—all that began with tiny seed. At the same time this bed of soil, as I discover each week, has the potential of producing the undesirable—the things I don't want. Weeds and grass and weeds and weeds. I pull them and discard them. They keep coming back. The potential of good and bad, the seed of good and bad, exists within my flower bed. The rain falls on the just and the unjust plant—and both have the potential to become something big. Jesus calls this the wheat and the tares. They both grow up in the same garden. Truth is, they both grow up in us.

We have the potential to grow to become something big—bad or good—if we allow it.

In Richard Evans's masterful three-volume history of Germany's Third Reich he describes the background of many of the main characters in that dark time of history. One such character was Rudolph Hoss, who grew to become the commandant of Auschwitz. We all know the story of Auschwitz and the evil perpetrated there, but where did it begin? It began with a little boy, Rudolph Hoss, who was raised a devout Roman Catholic. He went to church every Sunday. The seed of the kingdom being planted . . . but the seed of evil planted in him when he had gone to confession and confessed a secret sin to the priest, —but the priest later betrayed his confidence and told of the sin. Humiliation followed. The seed was planted. The young boy gave up his faith, and a bad and destructive weed was allowed to grow.

Within each of us is the start of something big. Seeds are planted all the time— and that can be good news and that can be bad news.

We understand that when Jesus talks about the kingdom of God, he would have us look honestly at our lives and see that our souls are soils—and that within each human heart is a fertile soil for good and bad seed. Anything can grow inside the human heart, and it doesn't take much for something small to turn into something big.

You've had it happen to you. Maybe when you were a child you received a certain kindness from an adult—and that kindness made you want to become kind. How many nurses have I talked to who said the reason for becoming a nurse was that as children they had to be hospitalized, and in that very scary and often painful place, a nurse came to the side of their bed and administered kindness and grace and healing. The small seed was planted, and it grew to become something big.

I am one of three brothers to become pastors. Aside from the fact that it was the only work we could get, I attribute the origin of our pastoral callings to the dinner table where the three of us sat, with our pastor father at one end and our mother at the other. Ninety-nine percent of the dinners I ate at that table had those two at either end, sowing good seed. My dad was a very busy pastor, but he sat at that table every night. He made being a pastor look like a pretty good job, and he was right.

A dear friend of mine, a businessman, recounts how his early years of schooling were not a time when he, should we say, applied himself, and he almost threw away his chances of preparing for a career. But one professor took a chance and admitted him into his program because the professor saw the potential of the soil. The seed was planted, and this now very successful entrepreneur frequently looks back and sees how the whole thing started—with the small seed of faith planted in his soul.

Small things become big things.

But we must be aware that it works the other way.

Remember the little seed of jealousy that drifted into your life; it took root and caused you to do something so silly and stupid and shameful. It made you into something you swore you would never become.

Or the little seed of anger that began to germinate in you a long time ago when a parent slighted you, or did worse to you, and you kept holding on to that anger. You did not pull that weed from your garden, and it has now grown and flowered and brought hurt upon so many within the reach of your branches.

Or the bitterness that stemmed from some failure in your life that you are wont to blame on someone else: "If it hadn't have been for so-and-so . . . If hadn't been for something that happened." You grow bitter, and before you know it, the bitterness has taken over the whole garden.

What's the point here? The point is that you and I have within us the start of something beautiful—big and beautiful. We have within us the start of the kingdom of God. It begins with the word of grace that comes from the Father, through the Son, and accompanied by the Holy Spirit. God is so eager to give us the seed of the kingdom amid all the other seeds that the world blows about. But it takes us drawing close to the sower—coming into communion with the farmer who wishes to plant the harvest . . . to receive the broadcast of the seed from his hand. It means drawing close to those places where the seed is at hand, so that our chances grow of receiving it. Warning: That place may not be in front of your TV. It may not be in the coolest of the crowds. It may not be with the people making the most money. It may be on your knees beside your bed in prayer. It may be in fellowship with your brothers and sisters in Christ. It may be through the sweat and toil of a mission trip. It may be inside the pages of your Bible somewhere, somewhere close to the sower.

Anthony de Mello tells the story about the farmer whose corn always took the first prize at the state fair, and how he always had the habit of sharing his best corn seed with all the farmers in his neighborhood. When asked why he would let others have his prize seed he said, "It's really a matter of self-interest. The wind picks up the pollen and carries it from field to field. So if my neighbors grow inferior corn, the cross-pollination brings down the quality of my own corn. This is why I am concerned that they plant only the best."

It matters where you plant your field.

It matters where we plant ourselves from day to day. Where we place ourselves— where we direct our minds, our eyes, our thoughts, our emotions—matters. All sorts of seed are blowing about, and our souls are the soil. Small things become big things. I suppose that's why, from the dark dungeons of a Roman jail, where your mind can wander to all sorts of conclusion, the apostle Paul writes, "Whatever is true, whatever is honorable, whatever is just, whatever is pure, whatever is pleasing, whatever is commendable, if there is any excellence, and if there is anything worthy of praise, think about these things, and the God of peace will be with you."

That the good seed might grow and the bad seed might die, and that God's small things might become God's big things.

CTHE SET OF THE SAILS

Luke 8:22–25

PAUL ECKMAN IS an American psychologist who has been voted one of *Time* magazine's one hundred most influential people in the world. Eckman has risen to that rank in part due to his research on emotions. Most of his life's research has focused upon the emotions that human beings experience and how those emotions are revealed in our facial expressions. In his study of emotions Eckman has been able to categorize six basic emotions that human beings feel: fear, anger, disgust, sadness, surprise, and happiness. If we feel anything, what we feel will likely fall into one of those categories.

The interesting thing about these six human emotions is that four of them are negative: fear, anger, disgust, and sadness. One—surprise—is neutral; you can be pleasantly surprised or negatively surprised. Only one emotion is positive: happiness. Of the emotions that humans can feel, one sixth are purely positive. Two thirds are negative. If we are bound to feel some way over the course of our lives, we are bound to feel bad. Fear, anger, disgust, and sadness tip the scale toward humans feeling bad, and each of these bad emotions is related to our response to the outside world. We fear something will happen to us. We are angry that something has happened to us. We are disgusted by what we have seen and heard, and we are sad because of our perception of the way things are. Human beings are wired to be responsive to external stimuli, and external stimuli is often felt as a threat, an unwelcome intruder. The result is that we are likely to feel afraid, angry, disgusted, or sad.

Another scientist—a neuroscientist named Richard Davidson (another one of *Time*'s one hundred most influential people)—has focused his brain research on whether we can train our brains to feel one emotion over another. Davidson has been particularly curious to see whether we can exercise our brains—like we would exercise the rest of our bodies—in such a way to tip the balance away from negative emotion to the positive emotion of happiness.

It's called *neuroplasticity*. Is the brain malleable enough to take our hardwiring and rewire it so that the current of emotion changes from negative to positive? Davidson has researched the brains of spiritually contemplative people—monks in particular, those who commit their lives to an almost unending practice of contemplating the divine. He has found that their systematic contemplative practice—the daily exercise of concentrating on the beauty and wonder of God—actually changes their brain functions such that they are able to experience to a larger degree the emotion of happiness. Even when the external world is sending a negative message, or if we are inside a negative situation, the brain is still able to continue to experience the emotion of happiness.

Maybe the apostle Paul had already come to this conclusion long before there was "neuroscience," long before they could take pictures of the brain, long before they thought about the six emotions. The apostle Paul writes to the Philippians from a Roman prison—an external world that was bound to create some negative emotion,

> Rejoice in the Lord always. Again I will say, Rejoice. . . . In everything by prayer and supplication with thanksgiving let your requests be made known to God. And the peace of God, which surpasses all understanding, will guard your hearts and your minds in Christ Jesus. . . . Whatever is true then, whatever is honorable, whatever is just, whatever is pure, whatever is pleasing, whatever is commendable, if there is any excellence, and if there is anything worthy of praise, think about these things. . . . I have learned to be content with whatever I have.

Remember, he writes this from a Roman prison.

Lest we think that this is some ancient guy telling us in his ancient way to simply put on a happy face, listen to what Paul says. He seems to understand what the great mystics and contemplatives have come to understand over the ages, and what scientists are just beginning to figure out today: "Whatever is true, whatever is honorable, whatever is just, whatever is pure, whatever is pleasing, whatever is commendable, if there is any excellence and if there is anything worthy of praise, think about these things."

He doesn't say, "When things go bad, flip on the happy switch." He says, "How you respond to the conditions around you are determined largely by what you have been thinking all along. And what you have been thinking all along is governed by how intentional you are over the things you're thinking about."

That knowledge could have been some help to the disciples on the boat in the Sea of Galilee. Mark tells us that Jesus and the disciples stepped into a boat to cross the sea, and all of a sudden a windstorm arose. The whitecaps formed and the water started to swamp, and they were straining with their oars and panicking. They were afraid—not to mention angry, disgusted, sad, and surprised. What they're not is happy. They are definitely not happy.

But Jesus is happy, at least happy enough to stay sleeping in the boat. We could say he was a deep sleeper, but I think Mark the storyteller wants us to see that the sleeping Jesus is content. He is not afraid or angry. He is resting. He is at peace.

The disciples say—"Yo, Jesus [loose translation of the Greek], don't you care? Don't you get it? Don't you understand that you are supposed to be afraid with us? You are supposed to be angry with us. You are supposed to be disgusted with us!"

"No," says Jesus, "because I've been thinking. I've been thinking about whatever is true, whatever is honorable, whatever is just, whatever is pure, whatever is pleasing, whatever is commendable, whatever is excellent, whatever is worthy of praise. These are the things I am thinking."

I know what you are thinking: when there's a storm at sea Jesus is not the guy you want with you in the boat. You want an oarsman. You want a seasoned sailor. You want somebody swift of foot. You want someone who is going to worry and be afraid and *do something about it*. You don't want anyone sleeping.

Eugene Peterson reminds us of a scene in *Moby Dick*—one of those scenes in which the crew of the *Pequod* is giving chase to the great mammoth whale. Captain Ahab is barking orders. Sailors are dashing across the deck. The cosmic conflict between good and evil is joined. The demonic sea monster meets the morally outraged man. But one man on the crew lies perfectly still. He has no oar in his hand, no lines to pull, no wheel to steer, no sails to trim. He is still in the midst of chaos. He is the harpooner, quiet and poised and waiting. Melville writes, "To insure the greatest efficiency in the dart, the harpooners of this world must start to their feet out of idleness, and not out of toil."

None of us like that word "idleness." Maybe you do, but I sure don't. I like activity. I like getting up and doing things. I like taking matters into my own hands. I don't like sitting around. Sitting around is for sissies. I like *Go, go, go*. But *Go, go, go* doesn't get me thinking about the things that are true and honorable and just and pure and pleasing and commendable and excellent and worthy of praise. The hardwiring doesn't get rewired because I've left no time to do the rewiring.

So much wants to take us away from the thinking and pondering and praying and glorifying. So much wants to keep us afraid and angry and sad and disgusted.

The people of God encountered this struggle when they went back to Palestine. They have their heads on straight. They know that if anything is going to get built, the first thing to build is the temple, because in the temple we think about God. In the temple we read and listen to the word of God. In the temple we consider the things of God. Because God is goodness. God is the author of every good and perfect gift. God is the source of honor and purity and justice and excellence. We go to the temple to worship and to pray and to ponder the things of God. Because here is where our peace is. Here is where our joy is. Here is where our happiness is.

But Jerusalem has enemies, forces that want to pull the people of Israel away from the temple—away from worship, away from thinking of the honorable and the just and the pure. Forces want Jerusalem afraid and angry and sad.

Because that's what life is, isn't it? Life is filled with all these windstorms, gales, and whitecaps, and we strain at the oars. But in the church we find Jesus. In the hull of the ship we find Jesus. And in Jesus we find peace, contentment, joy, and power. Yet inexplicable we say to ourselves that now is not the time to spend with Jesus. Let's wait for the storm to subside, for the wind to die down.

But the wind never dies down. The calendar never really clears. The phone—especially the cell phone—never stops ringing. And if we wait for all that to happen before we turn to Jesus, before we start building the temple, before we make the time to think about the things of honor and purity and justice—then we never do it at all. The result? The emotions of our life stay on the minus side. Fear and anger and sadness and disgust win the day in our hearts.

In 1960 a federal judge ordered the white schools of New Orleans to allow African American children to attend. Great conflict arose. Hate, anger, and fear filled the papers and the streets and the radios and the TVs. It fell on little ten-year-old Ruby Bridges to be the only African American child to attend the William T.

Frantz School. Outside the school's front door were hundreds of people uttering all the words of fear and anger and hate and disgust. But little Ruby seemed oblivious to it all as she walked to the door, escorted by federal marshals. All the child psychologists met with her to see what lasting damage all this activity was having on the poor young girl. But Ruby seemed happy. She seemed content. She seemed like a young girl of fortune. One day her teacher saw her approach the school, again barraged by epithets unrepeatable in a sermon. The teacher watched as Ruby stopped and began speaking in the face of all this venom poured upon her. When she entered the school, the teacher asked Ruby what she was speaking about with all those hateful people. She said, "Oh, I was just praying. I was just praying." What were you praying about, Ruby? "Oh, I was praying for them. My Sunday school teacher told me that they need praying for. So I prayed for them. I prayed for God to help them."

"Whatever is true, whatever is honorable, whatever is just, whatever is pure, whatever is pleasing, whatever is commendable, whatever is excellent, whatever is worthy of praise . . . think about these things."

Ella Wheeler Wilcox put it this way:

> But to every mind there openeth,
> A way, and way, and away,
> A high soul climbs the highway,
> And the low soul gropes the low,
> And in between on the misty flats,
> The rest drift to and fro.

> But to every man there openeth,
> A high way and a low,
> And every mind decideth,
> The way his soul shall go.

> One ship sails East,
> And another West,
> By the self-same winds that blow,
> 'Tis the set of the sails
> And not the gales,
> That tells the way we go.

Like the winds of the sea
Are the waves of time,
As we journey along through life,
'Tis the set of the soul,
That determines the goal,
And not the calm or the strife.

WRITTEN ALL OVER
THEIR FACES

John 20:1–18

How you live your life has a lot to do with who you think is in it with you.

In every elementary school in America there resides a bully. Arthur McGill Elementary School had a bully. I found that out the hard way. For the life of me I cannot recall his name, but I can see his face—even today. I can see it because his face was in my mind every night when I went to sleep for a few weeks when I was in the second grade. He bullied me, he picked on me, he threatened to pound me. I worried a great deal about him.

One night at the dinner table, my brother sitting across from me likely saw the bullied-worried expression on my face. He spoke up: "What's wrong with you?" Older brothers have this nice, gentle pastoral way about them.

"Nuthin'," I said. I peeked over at my mother, and she was looking at me with that motherly look: "I know you're lying." One look at her, and tears started down my cheeks.

"What's wrong with you?" my brother again sensitively inquired. I explained about the bully. When I was done, Mother gave her motherly advice. "Well, you just ignore him." Of course, that never works. But after dinner my brother took me aside and explained that this bully's home was on my brother's paper route. My brother knew where he lived. My brother instructed me that the next time the bully tried to do anything to me, I was to explain to him that I had a brother in tenth grade and that he knew where he lived, and that all I needed to do was say the word, and there would be consequences.

I don't remember all of what happened after that. I'm pretty sure that bully bullied me again. I suspect I played my older brother trump card. And since I have no recollection of getting beat up, I imagine that the bully decided to pick on someone else, someone without an older sibling who knew where he lived.

But what I do remember is how I felt that night when I went to bed after talking with my brother, and how I felt when I went to school the next day. I felt different. I felt like I was not alone. I felt like someone was there with me.

How you live your life has a lot to do with who you think is in it with you. I suspect that's one of the fundamental human needs: to know if there is someone, anyone, with me on this.

When I marry a couple in front of this sanctuary, they are satisfying that basic human need—the need to know that someone is with me on this.

When businesspeople make a business deal, they want and need to know who is with them on this.

When making a loan, banks often want to know if the borrower has someone "with them" on it.

When playing sports, a kid wants to know if someone up there in the stands is with them in the game.

How you live your life has a lot to do with who you think is in it with you.

I love the story about Atley Donald. You diehard Yankee fans know who Atley Donald was. Back in 1939 Atley was a young pitcher trying to make his way onto the Yankees. He had been invited to spring training, and none other than Joe DiMaggio took an interest in the young pitcher. But it was also during spring training that Atley hurt his arm. When it came time for the season to begin and for the Yankees to go north to New York, Atley was held back to get his arm back in shape. The Yankees were still not sure he would make the team. Just before they left, Joe DiMaggio approached Atley Donald and said, "You know, while you're here in Florida you need to ride in style like a Yankee, so I want you to have the keys to my Cadillac convertible. Take it wherever you want while you're down here and getting better, and when you are done here and you are ready to come to New York, you just give the keys to this gentleman and he will see that the car gets to New York." Atley Donald was in shock. He couldn't do it. He couldn't handle the thought of riding around in Joe DiMaggio's car. He told DiMaggio to keep the keys. A couple of days later the Yankees boarded the train for New York, and when Atley Donald returned to his hotel he found an envelope with the keys to the Cadillac and a note from DiMaggio that read, "Atley, a Yankee should ride in style. I believe in you."

Within a few weeks Atley's arm got better, and he was called up to Yankee Stadium. If you check the record books for Major League Baseball in 1939, you'll find that a rookie pitcher named Atley Donald set the record for the most consecutive victories for a rookie pitcher. Twelve consecutive victories. And in every one of those victories, a gentleman in centerfield named DiMaggio was with him.

We all need someone with us.

This very phenomenon seems to be the only thing that begins to explain what took place in the lives of a very small group of people, the followers of Jesus, back in the early part of the first century. Scripture tells us that Jesus's followers were people pretty much like you and me. They had jobs, they had bills to pay, they had families to feed. They had a range of IQs, just like any group of people. They had hopes and fears, worries and dreams. But when the wheels started to come off Jesus's ministry in that week we call Holy Week, it turned out that what the followers of Jesus didn't have was Jesus. After Jesus's arrest, after Jesus's death on the cross . . . they had no Jesus. All these visions for the kingdom of heaven, all these ideas about making disciples of all nations, all these dreams of spreading the good news—but no Jesus. He was gone. He was not with them. And without Jesus with them, they run, they scatter, they desert, they betray, they deny, and in the end they cower inside a room hiding from those who might threaten them. Living life with Jesus is one thing; living life afterward without him is something else entirely. Now they were living life without him, and it wasn't going so well. They were on their own—not a good place to be.

On your own is never a good place to be. We've all been there at one time or another, when we felt like it was us against the world—on our own to face the boss, make a living, pass the test, face life without a spouse. Even on our own in the middle of a crowd is not such a great place to be. For most American kids, their and their parents' number-one goal is to get "on their own." "You need to be on your own," I remember my father saying to me. But truly being on your own is never a good place to be. We can end up doing some pretty foolish things when we are on our own. We grow afraid and we worry when we think we are on our own.

There's Mary Magdalene, on her own, going to the tomb of Jesus. So convinced was she that she was alone that when she saw the tomb empty—and when she saw the angels in white, and when she saw Jesus himself standing in front of her—it was as if she was seeing nothing. Could a person possibly be going on her way and have

Jesus standing in front of her, evidences of his resurrection all around her, and yet she cannot see it? Of course, if she thinks she is on her own.

Yet by virtue of his grace or his voice, when Jesus speaks to Mary and calls her name, she is able to see that she is not what she thought she was. She is not on her own. Jesus is with her. And he's not just with her in some ethereal, new-agey kind of way. He is physically with her. The tomb is empty, and Jesus is speaking her name. He is really with her. This isn't just a feeling or a sense. The resurrected Jesus is standing in front of her.

That's why Easter is so important. Easter is a historical event, not a story or a fable or a parable or a myth. Easter is the good news that says that Jesus is alive—and not only is he alive but he is with us. Easter tells us that we are not on our own.

My guess is that when Mary ran back to tell the disciples that she had seen the Lord, she probably didn't need to say a thing. I suspect the news was written all over her face. That's how real this event was. And it wasn't just Mary, but eventually the rest of them, too.

The two men walking to Emmaus, do you remember that story? The resurrected Jesus walks alongside them, and for the longest time—even though they converse with him and dine with him—they do not recognize him. But by virtue of his grace, their eyes are opened and they see him. From then on, it must have been written all over their faces. Then the rest of the disciples turn away from being those fleeing, abandoning, betraying, denying, cowering would-be followers, and within a matter of days they are preaching in the streets, casting out demons, raising lame men to their feet.

So much of life has to do with who you believe is with you.

The Israelites had no doubt when Moses came down from the mountain. They knew he had climbed the summit to receive God's law, but how could they have known that when he came down from the mountain, the fact that God was with him—the event and reality of God's presence—would be written all over his face?

Who is with you today? Who is *really* with you? If you are one of the fortunate ones, you might be able to point to a few people in your life and count them as those who are with you. A small group of friends, perhaps. A few family members. Some brothers and sisters in Christ. Maybe you have a big brother. Maybe you have a Joe DiMaggio. But who is really with you?

Who's with you in the middle of the night when you are worried and you can't get to sleep? Who's with you when a significant relationship in your life—maybe even your marriage—falls apart? Who's with you when you have to make a major decision and you don't know quite what to do? Who's with you when the doctor says, "We have to run some more tests"?

Maybe you're not sure who's with you. You might be in one of those seasons of life when you wonder if you are on your own. But despite whether your circle is big or small—or whether you have no circle at all—it all changes with today. A scared woman alone walked to a tomb expecting to see nothing, expecting that she would be just as much on her own when she left as when she came. That scared, alone young woman came to a tomb and found it empty—and she discovered that the Jesus whom she thought had left her was the Jesus who was now with her. Now she wasn't alone. Now she could run—not run away, but run to the disciples and become the first Christian preacher when she said, "I have seen the Lord."

In the waning days of World War II, in a German prison in Schonberg, Germany, a group of prisoners waited for what they were sure would be the day of their execution. It was the Sunday after Easter, and as they gathered there in fear and trembling, it did not look like Easter, nor feel like Easter, nor smell like Easter. But one of them, a professor named Dietrich Bonhoeffer, stood forth and proclaimed that it was the Sunday after Easter, the first Sunday of Eastertide. Then he read these words: "Blessed be the God and Father of our Lord Jesus Christ . . . for by his great mercy we have been born anew to a living hope through the resurrection of Jesus Christ from the dead." Then he preached, although not for long. No one remembers quite what he said. But those who were there do remember one thing. They remembered his demeanor—Dietrich Bonhoeffer's peaceful countenance. It was as if Jesus was with him. It was written all over his face.

When their little service was over, the guards came and took him away. It was the last time they would ever see him. His final words? "This is the end, but for me, just the beginning."

That's what Easter is, isn't it? Just the beginning. For Mary, for the disciples, for every one of Jesus's followers. It's just the beginning. It's what happens when you believe—I mean, *really* believe—that Jesus is with you. It changes things because it means you are never on your own. The world is full of bullies and forces that want to pull you down. The world is full of pressures and deadlines and illnesses and unexpected events. And the world wants to convince you that you are on your own, but Easter changes that. Easter means that you are never on your own.

"For blessed be the God and Father of our Lord Jesus Christ . . . for by his great mercy we have been born anew to a living hope through the resurrection of Jesus Christ from the dead."

The Lord is risen!

The Lord is risen indeed!

ᴄʟʜᴇ ᴄᴏᴍꜰᴏʀᴛs ᴏꜰ ᴘᴏsᴛᴘᴏɴᴇᴍᴇɴᴛ

Mark 1:1–8

THE DROP APPEARED to be ten thousand feet. A glance down felt like staring into the abyss. The consideration of jumping was like choosing certain death. This was what my nine-year-old heart and mind felt as I stood on top of the high dive at the St. Clair Shores public pool. All my buddies had been jumping and diving off the high dive for weeks, but I had held back, favoring the medium diving board as my comfort zone. But then came the day when I stood in line for the high dive. With every second as the line inched forward, my heart pounded harder. When I reached the ladder, I stepped away and feigned the need to do something else. Then I got back in line again.

This time when I got to the ladder, I began to climb. When you begin to climb the ladder you've just about reached the point of no return. I climbed the twelve hundred steps of the ladder until I made the summit. I began to walk what felt like the plank. Halfway out, I hesitated. My friends in line down below were their usual supportive selves. "Come on, McConnell, you baby. You sissy. Jump, you wimp!" Very supportive.

I resumed my walk to death, slowly. "McConnell's a sissy. McConnell's a sissy." What great friends I had.

Finally I got to the end of the board, and there it was. The yawning chasm. The plunge to permanent injury. This was it, the moment of truth. I turned around. Laughter from down below. What was worse? Humiliation if I climb back down the ladder, or one and a half seconds of terror if I jump?

"McConnell's a sissy."

I turned back around and went to the edge of the dive. I looked over at the life-guard sitting on her stand. A high school girl. Blond and tanned. She saw my look of terror. She smiled and motioned with her head to jump. Against my better judgment, I cast myself into the deep . . . the first of five hundred times I jumped off that high dive.

Life is filled with those moments, isn't it? Moments when the decision to do one thing or the other feels like a jump off the high dive . . . or the edge of the Grand Canyon. And the question is: Do I jump, or do I climb back down the ladder?

Decisions: College, marriage, buying a house, having a baby, taking a job, changing careers, starting a new business, moving . . . Do I jump or climb back down the ladder? Do I take a risk or play it safe? Do I let my heart race and my temples sweat, or do I ease back into my recliner and not trouble myself?

There is something soul searching about these times.

Something was soul searching, too, about the time when John the Baptist was at the river Jordan. He was preaching a baptism of repentance for the forgiveness of sins. He was shouting down the scribes and the Pharisees, heralding a new way of living into the covenant of God. It wasn't about just following the rules; it was about what happens inside a person's heart. It was about repentance—renouncing the old ways and choosing a new way of life. It was about giving yourself away to God and to your neighbor. "Come down into the river," John said. "Be baptized. Leave behind the old life. A new way is coming. Prepare the way of the Lord. Take the plunge. Be baptized with the Holy Spirit."

Say whatever you want about John—he was a kook, Elijah, a troublemaker, a religious fanatic, and more—one thing for certain is that he was soul searching. You had to search your soul to decide whether you were going to walk into the river.

Walking into the river, or walking across the river, was crossing a point of no return. That's what the river Jordan was for the people of Israel: the crossing point, stepping into God's future. When the people of Israel left Egypt, their first journey across the wilderness was not so long, just a couple of years. They reached the edge of Canaan and sent spies to look over the river Jordan . . . and they saw giants in the promised land. With one exception, the spies said, "We can't cross over. It's the point of no return. It's too risky. Best to stay in the wilderness. Best to buy some time. Best to postpone." So the people of Israel searched their souls and retreated and wandered for another thirty-eight years. That's what happens when you don't choose: You wander.

Carole Shields, in her wonderful novel *The Stone Diaries*, writes these exquisite lines: "The larger loneliness of our lives evolves from our unwillingness to spend ourselves, stir ourselves. We are always damping down our inner weather, permitting ourselves the comforts of postponement."

A lot of people like to play their lives that way, with the comforts of postponement. "You know I really should do this, but let me wait on it. I have [my job, my kids, my obligations, my questions, my fears, my worries]. I will choose the comforts of postponement."

John stands in the same river and says, "Come on down into the river, and choose a new way of life. Become a disciple. Receive the Holy Spirit that the Messiah will bring and become a new creation. Search your souls."

When the Spanish conquistador Hernando Cortés brought his fleet of ships to the shores of Mexico to begin his conquest of new lands for his motherland, Spain, the first order of the general when the men emptied out of the ships and onto the land was "Burn the ships." Burn the armada. Now the men knew there was no turning back, no climbing back down the ladder, no comforts of postponement. They were on the other side of the river.

Discipleship is like that. It's really the first thing to consider when we think about Jesus's call. Deciding to be a disciple is just that: a decision. And it's not just a decision; it becomes *the* decision. That's why John is standing in the river. He is inviting us to the point of no return, into the future of God—and the future of God, the life of discipleship, is not something you do occasionally, when it feels right. It's just something you do. It's all in. It's burning the ships.

We would expect no less. Nothing important begins with a mealymouthed request. We wouldn't be here this morning if John had stood in the river and said, "You know, if you want to, come on down into the river. But only on the days you want to. You don't have to do it all the time, only when it works into your schedule. Only when it feels convenient. You can kind of go back and forth if you want." We wouldn't be here if John had asked us just to come halfway.

When I played sports and signed up for the team—it didn't matter what the team was, football or basketball or track—it would have sounded strange on the first day if the coach had said, "We have this season ahead of us, and we intend to win a championship, and every afternoon we are going to practice. Come to the practice whenever you like, whichever and however many days you prefer. Come when you can. Play when you like."

Nothing important begins with a mealymouthed request. Jesus knows us better. He says that no one can serve two masters. He'll love the one and hate the other, hate the one or love the other. It's all in or all out.

Boris Pasternak, the author of *Doctor Zhivago*, wrote,

> The great majority of us are required to live a life of constant, systematic duplicity. Your health is bound to be affected if, day after day, you say the opposite of what you feel, if you grovel before what you dislike and rejoice at what brings you nothing but misfortune. Our nervous system isn't just a fiction, it's a part of our physical body, and our soul exists in space and is inside us, like the teeth in our mouth. It can't be forever violated with impunity.

It is, perhaps, the most gracious thing that John the Baptist does for us: to save us from the duplicities of our lives that take us off course. He invites us to choose the one path, to jump into the one river, to go in one direction, to follow the one Savior.

I can't wait until January ends and the interminable commercials for diet plans come off the air—most of them anyway. But for people who want or need to lose a few pounds, the truth of the matter is that you need a plan and to stick to the plan. It would be silly to hear someone say, "Here is what you can or cannot eat on the plan, but only on the days you feel like it." The scale would eventually prove the wrong-headedness of such an approach.

Nothing important begins with a mealymouthed request, and nothing important happens until you take the jump.

You're either all in or all out.

This outlook might explain the situation when Jesus is walking the dusty trails of Palestine, and he sees a man and says, "Follow me."

The man says, "Let me go back home and say good-bye."

Jesus responds, "No one who puts a hand to the plow and looks back is fit for the kingdom of God." Sounds sort of harsh. Nothing mealymouthed about the Savior. "Time to jump into the river," Jesus says. No dipping toes. No one foot in and one foot out. Time to jump off the board or climb down the ladder—the thrill of the leap or the comforts of postponement.

That comes down to a very personal and individual decision. Dietrich Bonhoeffer, in his landmark book *The Cost of Discipleship*, wrote that through the call of Jesus each of us become individuals, because we can only make that decision on our own. "Christ makes us individuals," Bonhoeffer wrote, "by calling us."

Soul searching? Yes. But I promise that once you decide—once you leave behind the ladder, once you leave behind the comforts of postponement, once you jump—what awaits you are the enveloping and rolling waters of the mercies and purposes of God.

The Chances of Getting Lost

Luke 15:1–10

WHAT ARE THE chances of getting lost?

When I was eight years old I was invited to attend my friend Earl's eighth birthday party. Earl was one of my best friends. Seven or eight of us boys were invited to a party at his house, and when we arrived Mrs. Henderson suggested we go out and take a little walk around the block while she finished up the preparations for the party. We did, but the walk turned into something more. One thing led to another, and someone suggested a neat playground to play at—and thought he knew where that playground might be. We made a couple of wrong turns, but we finally figured out where it was. We took some time to play, and then we realized that the sun was starting to go down and maybe we should make our way back home. Remember, this was just supposed to be a walk around the block. We were now gone at least an hour.

We began our way back, but we didn't know where we were going. It was getting darker now, real dark. We made one bad turn that led to another bad turn—and we still didn't know where we were going. Now it was completely dark, and we were getting scared. We kept walking. Before we knew it we began to recognize some houses and some street names, and finally we got back to Earl's house. When we walked up the driveway we couldn't figure out why the police car was there. When we walked into the house we couldn't figure out why all our parents were there. Never have I seen expressions of such joy and relief and anger all wrapped into one as I did in Mrs. Henderson's expression.

Needless to say, that was the end of the party.

What are the chances of getting lost? Eight-year-old boys can do it pretty good.

In Disney World, where over a hundred thousand people mill around the grounds each day—over a hundred thousand!—they know that the chances of getting lost or separated are real good. Every Disney cast member knows this, and they know where the lost children log is. They know the exact procedure for helping lost people, because they know that the chances of getting lost in a sea of one hundred thousand people is very, very high.

I have a friend who pastors a church in Queens, New York. It's a church he started over twenty years ago in a pretty rough-and-tumble area, and it is now one of the most amazing spiritual communities I've experienced. Pete tells me that people from at least 50 different countries worship there on any given Sunday—the richest of the rich and the poorest of the poor. I once asked Pete why he decided to start a church in, of all places, Queens, New York? He said to me, "Steve, do you have any idea in a city like New York—a city of 8 million people—do you have any idea how easy it is to get lost?"

I knew that he wasn't talking about directions and street names, but about getting lost in a real way. He was talking about the millions of people who step off planes and buses and trains into New York with the hope of finding themselves, or at least with the hope of leaving something else behind. People want to make their mark. Instead, of course, a mark is made upon them. In their effort to be found, they get lost. To be freed, they get bound. To survive, they sell themselves. Pete says that he wanted to start a church where lost people could be found.

One of the central messages of Jesus's life and ministry and teaching is very simple, yet profound: In this world of ours, the chances of getting lost are enormous—not just physically lost, but, more important, spiritually lost.

Any parent knows what this is all about. You don't raise children in this world without giving a whole lot of thought to the possibility of them getting spiritually or emotionally lost out there. Parents talk a lot about their kids getting into the wrong or the right crowd, and it's all out of concern of whether they will get lost, whether they will find their way in the world.

Jesus says that the chances of getting lost in this world are pretty good. In fact, that's at the root of the debate he has with the Pharisees and the scribes. The Pharisees and the scribes see Jesus sitting around and eating with the tax collectors and sinners—all the bad people, according to some. When Jesus sees that the scribes and Pharisees are all hot and bothered by this, he begins to tell them stories about things and people who get lost. And in telling these stories, Jesus is explaining that the real issue when it comes to the kingdom of God is not whether people out there are bad or good, or smart or dumb, or lucky or unlucky; the central issue of the kingdom is whether they simply might be lost—because the chances are very good, according to Jesus, that in this big world of ours, a lot of people are going to get lost. For whatever reason, enormous amounts of people do not know where they are or where they are going in the world of the Spirit.

Jesus tells the scribes and Pharisees a story about the searching shepherd. They know what he's talking about; a good shepherd is keenly aware that some sheep are likely going to get lost, for whatever reason. To know this is to always be on the lookout. The good shepherd knows of lost sheep out there not because he's counted and recounted the flock and come up with ninety-nine out of a hundred. The good shepherd knows there's a strong likelihood that some lost sheep is out there somewhere—either from his flock or someone else's. The good shepherd doesn't look for a bad sheep or a good sheep, nor a smart sheep or a dumb sheep—just lost sheep.

We also know what Jesus is talking about. The possibility is enormous that lost people are not far from our reach. We've seen them; we know who they are—perhaps a person who has lost purpose in life, or a person lost in an addiction, lost in a bad relationship, lost as the result of some bad choices, lost in the midst of grief or illness, lost in the wrong crowd, lost in a moral malaise or spiritual emptiness.

Are we to judge them? Of course not. That's not what lostness is all about. You don't judge lost people. You find them and bring them back to their Creator. We don't judge; we just notice. We notice the people around us, and we look for the possibility of someone we know who may very well be lost and needs to be found. Like that woman sweeping out her house looking for that lost and valuable coin, we know how valuable these people are to the one who is telling the story. God turns the house inside out to find that coin, to find that soul, to find that person who has wandered off and waded in a little too deep.

There's a little bit of lostness in all of us. We are all yearning to go home. We're all yearning to find the place where the porch light is on and the anxious parent awaits.

Is this not the mission of the church? Is it not the mission of our church? To be the place with the porch light on? To have a heart for people who are lost? To have a heart for people who are outside of a relationship with God? Is this not a huge part of making and equipping disciples of Jesus Christ—to find a way, to discover a system, to devise a strategy by which lost people can get found? It all begins when you and I look at the world—when we look at our neighborhoods, our workplaces, our families, and even ourselves—and realize that there is a great chance that some people might be lost . . . and what they need is to be found. They need to be found in a relationship with the God who created them, the One from whom they came and to whom they will return.

George Carlin, that great theologian, used to talk about those things that human beings are most apt to misplace: car keys, glasses, widowed socks, and so on and so on. Carlin's thesis is that while we think we have misplaced them, instead they've gone to the "land of lost things." When you "lose" your car keys, you really didn't lose them; they just traveled off to the land of lost things. Your things stay there until they decide they want to be found again, and then they come back from the land of lost things and we find them. At the end of it all Carlin would say, "I wonder if heaven might be that place where we go to find all those things we've lost."

I think he might be right.

I have a severely retarded brother named Jimmy. Jimmy is four years older than me. He has never spoken a word in his life. He functions at about a three-year-old level. At the age of ten he was placed in a school for profoundly impaired children, and he has lived there ever since. He is now blind. Not long after Jimmy took residence in this school, one night the staff was making the evening bed checks, and Jimmy's bed was empty. They searched the room, but he wasn't there. They searched the wing, the floor, the building—he wasn't there. They called the police and the fire department. They searched the grounds, but he wasn't anywhere. They broadened the search to beyond the grounds. Perimeter searches commenced. Finally a fireman, walking gently through the woods, heard the sound of quiet crying. He raised his flashlight and found huddled next to a tree a little boy—a scared, shivering little boy who was lost. He wasn't bad; he was just lost, and he didn't have any words to say he was lost. They wrapped him in a blanket and took him home, and everyone rejoiced. The lost boy was found.

God also rejoices when lost boys get found—also when lost girls, lost women, and lost men get found. God gets really happy when that happens.

And that's why God makes churches: because the chances of getting lost in this world are enormous. Wouldn't it be nice to have a place where you can go and chances are you'd get found? A place where it doesn't matter what you look like nor where you've been? It doesn't even matter how you got lost or what you did while you were lost. We just know it's kind of scary when you get lost. We know, because there is a little bit of lostness in ourselves.

Where lost things get turned in, we call those places the "lost and found."

The Lost and Found: Sounds like a good name for a church.

Not Changing the Channel

Mark 3:20–35

There is a vitality,
a life force,
an energy,
a quickening that is translated through you
into action.
And because there is only one of you in all of time,
this expression is unique.
And if you block it,
it will never exist through any other medium
and be lost.
The world will not have it.
It is not your business to determine how good it is
nor how valuable
nor how it compares with other expressions.
It is your business to keep it yours
clearly and directly,
to keep the channel open. . . .

THOSE ARE THE words of the late Martha Graham, the great dancer and teacher of dance. She does not speak in the language of faith. I don't even know if she is a person of faith, but she does speak to something that lies at the core of our faith—something as foundational to our faith as the notion that a God exists. Take a moment and read her words again.

⁂

I AM NOT sure what Martha Graham means when she speaks of a vitality, a life force, an energy, or a quickening; it sounds a little new-agey to me. But I know that a God exists who is seeking to express himself to the world and to people in the world through the likes of people like you and me. Even if they start cloning us, there is and will always be only one of us in all of time, and God chooses our uniqueness through which to express himself to the world. We are the channels through which the spirit of God moves in God's effort to reach the world with the good news of his grace. Our job, according to Martha Graham, is to keep the channel open—not to block it, and certainly not to change it.

"We have gifts," writes the apostle Paul, "that differ according to the grace given us." This reality is as basic and true as our own existence: God has not simply put us here, but he has put us here with certain gifts and abilities. And he has not just given us gifts and abilities, but he has created us to be unique delivery systems. This unique delivery system is on this planet for a specific purpose—to bring about the kingdom of heaven, to receive grace and to be the channel through which grace is uniquely extended. Like an orchestra, each instrument is a channel for music, and the uniqueness of each instrument contributes to the greater sound. We are to keep the channel open, and certainly not to change it.

But as you know, these channels we are—these unique personalities that were knit together in our mothers' wombs—are under lots of pressure to change: to change the channel, to make us into people, personalities, and souls that we are not. From the moment we came out of the womb and were handed into our parents' arms, forces have been trying to change us. Some of it comes from good old basic parenting and teaching—people doing their best to guide us so that we don't drive off the cliff. Sometimes parenting is done well, and sometimes it's not. When we're growing up, our peers tend to want to shape the unique channels that we are by pressuring us to conform to a certain type of behavior, so that we can be accepted. Kids don't often know enough about themselves yet to claim their own souls and personality. Even growing up and growing older, there are subtle and not so subtle pressures to become someone different from whom we really are. Voices from the past or present play in our heads and say that we should not be the person we really are—that, for some reason, such a person won't be welcome in the kingdom of heaven.

Consider Jesus in this passage from Mark. It is early in Jesus's ministry, and he is saying some unique things about God and performing some unique ministry for God—enough out of the ordinary that it makes Jesus seem like an oddball. His mother and siblings decide they need to do something, since Jesus is not conforming to the norm. Time for an intervention. "He is out of his mind!" they say. "He is beside himself!" Translation: He is not living into our expectations for him. Imagine that: The Messiah is not living into our expectations. Isn't that what Messiahs do, live beyond our expectations? So even Jesus—the announced Messiah—is feeling the pressure to live into somebody else's expectations. Why don't you be a good Jewish boy and behave yourself?

Has that ever happened to you—you didn't live into somebody else's expectations? For some reason, someone thought you were not the right channel of grace? Or that you had to change to become more like what someone needed you to be? Say that God made you a French horn, but they want you to be a piccolo. No offense to piccolos, but the symphony gets a little dull when it's all piccolos.

God is trying to get to someone through you. God is trying to deliver a message to someone through the uniqueness of who you are, and that means there is a reason behind who you are. There is a reason for the uniqueness of your life. There is a reason for the gifts with which God has endowed you. A very small portion of that reason is for you to earn a living. God gives us gifts so we can be about our work and earn enough money to provide for our basic needs. That is God's secondary purpose for our gifts. The primary purpose behind our abilities and gifts is to be God's channel of love and grace for someone else's sake.

We are not accustomed to thinking that way. Most of us have learned that the chief end of man is to grow up, get an education, get a job, get a paycheck, get a place to live, get married, get some toys to play with, get old, and get buried—and that's what most people do. If they use their gifts, they go toward those ends. Getting a job so they can get paid so they can get some toys before they get buried. Never once is that used as a model for living in the Bible.

In page after page of the Bible, you find people whom God uses in very unique ways to be the channels of his grace and purpose for the sake of other people. Moses gets floated down the river as a baby, raised in Pharaoh's home, and ends up a fugitive in the wilderness. Why? So that God can use him to deliver the people from Egypt, through the wilderness, and into the promised land. Noah is a righteous man, good with his hands, likes to build things. Why? So that God can use him to save the human race. The apostle Paul is raised a zealous student of the law and fanatical defender of Judaism—even a persecutor of Christians. Why? So that he can become an amazing witness to the power of Jesus Christ and a bridge between the law of Moses and the grace of Christ. God gives us gifts and abilities primarily so that we can become the channels of his love and grace for someone else's sake. God is trying to get to someone through you.

When I was growing up in Michigan, one of the members of our church, Dr. Olsen, was a scientist somewhere. I'm really not sure what he did for a living. All I knew what that he was pretty smart when it came to scientific things. The reason I knew that? At church camp when I was in grade school, Dr. Olsen was the guy whom all us guys wanted to be around, because when you are a grade-school boy, you like things like bugs and turtles and snakes and scientific experiments. Dr. Olsen was into all those kinds of things, and he had a way of captivating our interest with all these bugs and turtles and snakes and experiments as a way of telling us about the amazing parts of God's creation and how wonderful God is to create such an amazing world as ours. I do not know what Dr. Olsen did for a living, but I do know what he did for a calling: open up the amazing wonders of God's world to a bunch of elementary school kids east of Detroit. And that's the point. It wasn't his living that mattered, it was his calling. God was getting to people through him.

Moses was a shepherd; that was his living. But we don't know him by his living; we know him by his calling. Peter was a fisherman. Paul was a tentmaker. Albert Schweitzer was a doctor. We don't remember these people by their livings, but by their callings.

What a shame if Jesus, after being scolded by his mother and siblings, had said, "Yeah, you're right. I need to shape up. Behave. Not say such outlandish things. Not call into the question the spirit of the times. I'll be a good little Jewish boy"? That wouldn't have just been a tragedy for Jesus but cataclysmic for the world.

Can you imagine God thinking the same thing? That our trying to be something we're not could ruin the whole orchestra?

Years ago, while walking through the Israel Museum in Jerusalem, I passed by a painting. I am not an artist, nor do I know much about art. I have never taken an art appreciation course. But when I passed by this painting I stopped and stared. The painting transfixed me with its beauty. It was a painting of a garden, and the colors and the use of light and the landscape it was capturing made for a truly spiritual experience—one of the moments of joy that C. S. Lewis talks about when you are simply lifted into a moment of spiritual longing. The painting was by Camille Pissarro—the grandfather of the French Impressionist movement—a pioneer painter who began a movement in painting first abhorred by the artist elite in France.

When I got home I researched Camille Pissarro to find out what led this man to create such beauty. I found that Camille had a father who owned his own shipping business, and his father wanted Camille to be a businessman. He wanted Camille to start work on the cargo docks and spend his life working his way up the business ladder and follow in the father's footsteps. But Camille was an artist. For years he conformed to his father's wishes and worked on the loading dock, but when he wasn't working on the loading dock he would steal away and paint. He would paint anything he could lay his eyes on, because that's what he was. Painting was his channel of grace. After years of doing this—hiding his light under a bushel—there came the time when Camille confronted his father and said, "Father, I am not a businessman, I am a painter." He left home and claimed his channel, and though he made hardly enough money to support himself and his family, and though he died a poor man, Camille Pissarro opened a channel. God's beautiful grace poured through, and generations and generations of people have stood before his gracious creations and—like that young man in the Israel Museum—found the joy of God.

And to think Camille could had stayed on the dock.

"When his family heard about Jesus, they went out to restrain him, for people were saying, 'He has gone out of his mind.'" It can happen to Messiahs. And it can happen as well to those who follow him.

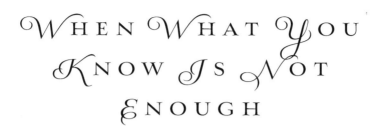

WHEN WHAT YOU KNOW IS NOT ENOUGH

Matthew 25:31–46

I READ ABOUT a man named John Williams who drove a bus in Milwaukee, Wisconsin. One particularly cold day—about ten degrees above zero—John Williams had a bus full of people. A woman was waiting at the next stop, so John Williams pulled over. The woman got on. She was pregnant, wearing tattered clothes and a worn, moth-eaten coat. On her feet were torn socks and no shoes. Ten degrees and no shoes. John Williams asked her how could she be out on such a cold day without any shoes. "No choice," the woman said. She explained that she was the mother of eight children and she had enough money to buy shoes for her children, but no more money to buy shoes for herself. She sat down.

When she sat down after her explanation, John Williams noticed a young man walking forward from the back of the bus. Frank Daily, age fourteen, approached the woman, stood in front of her, and handed her a pair of shoes. *How fortuitous*, thought John Williams. *Just when this woman needed a pair of shoes, there happened to be someone who had an extra pair*. Then he looked again in the rearview mirror and saw Frank Daily returning to his seat with bare feet. John Williams said he had trouble making it to the next bus stop because of the tears in his eyes. "Imagine," he said, "giving your shoes to someone else on a day like that."

Imagine, of course, is what we must do when wondering about our own actions if we were on that bus with John Williams and Frank Daily. Everyone on that bus stayed seated when they heard the woman's story, except for the fourteen-year-old boy. Would I have stood? Or would I stay seated? What could I imagine myself doing? What would lead to such an impulsive gesture of love and concern? Do I have that inside me?

Those same kind of questions might come to mind when we read and listen to this great story of Jesus's from the end of Matthew 25. This chapter of Matthew presents three stories that speak to the impending return of Jesus the Messiah. The first time it was the bridegroom making his way to the great wedding feast; some were prepared and some were not. The second time it was as the returning landowner and master coming back to settle accounts with his servants; some do well investing and some don't. This time the returning Messiah comes back as himself—bringing with him all the angels—and he gathers before him all the nations of the world. It's time for the final judgment, and like a shepherd, he separates the sheep from the goats. The Messiah/Shepherd does not ask who wants to be a sheep or a goat. He doesn't take a show of hands. In the end of time, that choice is no longer left to us. At some point, the side we're placed on is out of our hands. There will come the time when it is out of our hands—on which side we will be placed. We're no longer choosers, but the product of our choices.

That's a little unnerving.

Look also at the criterion by which the Messiah/Shepherd determines the sheep and the goats. Everyone is surprised, because they discover that the returning Messiah has been appearing to them all along. He has come to them in the form of all those who are in need—the hungry and the thirsty and the estranged and the naked and the sick and the imprisoned. Jesus has walked into their lives under the guise of real and physical human need. "Whatever you have done to the least of these, you have done it to me." Jesus has been showing up all along. He has been stepping onto the bus with bare feet when it's ten degrees outside. Some, like Frank Daily, have instinctively responded to the presence of Christ; others have remained seated. Some people live lives predisposed toward the hurts of the world, while others live lives of—in the words of Pink Floyd—a "turning away."

The criterion for whether we go to the right or the left is what we do when Christ appears in the form of the hungry, the thirsty, the estranged, the naked, the sick, and the imprisoned. The criterion is not what we think, feel, or say.

For most of us, this story of Jesus's return tells us something we already know. Even people who don't necessarily believe in Jesus know deep inside their brains that helping someone who needs help is a good thing. On the grand scale of human activity, at the top of most desired human activity is providing help to someone who needs it. A man is driving down the highway on his way to a meeting and sees a car broken down. He knows that helping the person broken down is more important than just about any meeting he is planning on attending. That's what the Good Samaritan story is all about.

We know this in our heads, but that's not always or often what we do. Maybe you're like me; I have it in my brain all the time that Jesus would be very pleased if I spent more time with the poor, the imprisoned, the estranged, the sick—but my life gets in the way. Does your life ever get in the way of what your brain is telling you to do? Do you ever have the coulda-woulda-shouldas? Do you fear that on that Milwaukee bus you might have stayed seated with your shoes on?

No matter what it thinks, the brain usually does not have the horsepower to get us to do what we know we should do. If logic was enough—and human beings are the great logicians—we'd be with the poor and the needy all day, every day. But the brain doesn't have the horsepower. The real horsepower comes from the heart. What we do in this life is an extension of what we hold in our hearts. Open a woman's calendar and you'll find what she holds in her heart. Open a man's checking account and you'll find what he holds in his heart. Open a window into a family's home and you'll find what they hold in their hearts. The heart governs what we do. "Where your treasure is, there will your heart be also."

I read a story about Demmy Salivas, who likes to cook for Christmas. She thinks about it for months and begins planning the menu weeks ahead of time. She hunts for recipes. She buys the cookbooks from the best chefs. Christmas dinner has to be perfect, because she's doing it for very special people: the residents of the Shelter Our Sisters Battered Women's Center in Northern New Jersey. Every Christmas she puts out the spread upon the finest tablecloths she can find. She corrals food from friends and neighbors and help from anyone who is willing to give their Christmas day to these women and their children. She wants it to be an unforgettable time of festivity. She'd rather be no place else, because the Shelter Our Sisters Shelter is where her heart is. How did her heart get there? She was once one of those women, fifteen years before, seeking shelter with her children, eating a TV dinner on Christmas. When she left the shelter and got her life back again, she began to do for them out of a deep and profound gratitude for what had been done for her. She wants to be there on Christmas, because for her there is no other place Christ would be on Christmas than in the lives of those frightened, battered women and children.

The gratitude she held in her heart for what had been done for her led her to be freed to do what needed to be done for others.

Might that not be the secret to it all—that our predisposition toward doing for others is born out of the thanksgiving held deep in our hearts for what has been done for us? One of the great spiritual truths confirmed in just about every page of Scripture is just that: our proclivity toward the needs of the world is commensurate to the amount of thanksgiving we hold in our hearts for what has been done for us.

You know the story of the old, old man whose neighbor noticed him planting something in his backyard. The neighbor went over to the old man and asked him what he was planting. "Oh, I'm planting a peach tree. I sure love peaches, so I thought I would plant a peach tree."

The neighbor tried to polite, but curiosity got the better of him. He asked, "It's great that you love peaches, but given your age it doesn't look like you're ever going to eat any peaches from this tree."

"Oh," said the old man, "this tree isn't for me. It just dawned on me that every peach I've ever eaten has been from someone else's tree. So now I realize that it's my turn to plant a tree for someone else."

Our response to the needs of the world doesn't come from the head; it comes from the heart. Our instinctive response to people who are hungry and thirsty and estranged and naked and sick and imprisoned is born out of a profound gratitude for what has already been done for us.

What has been done for you? It's probably a pretty easy list to make. Start when you were young. When you were two years old, did you clothe yourself? Did you cook your own meals? When you were ten, did you teach yourself? When you were fifteen and gave no one a reason to love you, just because you were fifteen, did someone go against the grain and love you anyway? When you were older, did someone employ you? Did someone befriend you? Did someone help you out of a jam? When you lost your job, did someone walk with you and give you a hand? That's just the beginning. As believers we can even go back to the beginning of it all when we were just microscopic zygotes in our mother's womb; we know that it was the finger of God knitting us together. It was not our idea to be born; the grand Creator with some grand design got us started. Think, then, of what happened on the cross when that same Creator looked at his broken creation—every little broken part of you and me—and said to himself that a new creation was in store and forgiveness was needed. Without our help, the Messiah strapped himself up on that cross and did what we could not do for ourselves—took our sin upon himself and forgave us free and clear.

Do you see what happens when you begin to hold in your heart all the thanks-givings of life—from the smallest to the greatest? When you train your heart upon all that has been done for you when you could not do for yourself, when your heart gets so filled with thanksgiving? Then you cannot help but to instinctively and impulsively give. Give to the hungry because you once were hungry, to the thirsty because you once were thirsty, to the estranged because you once were a stranger, to the naked because you once were naked, to the sick because you once were sick, and to the imprisoned because you once were imprisoned. You just can't help yourself.

Our salvation lies here, doesn't it? Not *up here*, but *down here*. Our salvation lies in that place where we finally make sense of it all—that it's all about not what we have done for ourselves but what has been done for us . . . in creation, in the cross, and in the 10 billion kindnesses that have come our way. Training our hearts upon all those things that have been done for us, filling our hearts to overflowing with thanksgiving . . . imagine what our lives would be?

Perhaps like Joseph Dutton: survivor of the American Civil War whose spiritual scars from the war led him to alcoholism, a broken marriage, and utter despair. Joseph Dutton's wrecked life was claimed along the way by gracious people and a gracious God. To make a very long story short, he found himself called to serve as a priest to the lepers of the infamous Molokai leper colony in Hawaii. For the remainder of his years he gave his life to those whom the world had cast away. When asked in his twilight years about God's call to such a forsaken place, the good father responded about his fellowship with the unclean, "Did ever one deserve so little and get so much?"

It is the secret to life, isn't it—the life now and the life beyond? Seeing how little we deserve and how much we've been given. Seeing these things is to see the Christ—the Christ within and the Christ in the guise of all who, like us, cannot help themselves.

CHECKING YOUR BLIND SIDE

2 Samuel 12:1–7

ONE OF THE great lessons in life I learned from Mr. Walny, my driver's education teacher. We've all had the lesson: Check your blind spot. The first time I got into a car to learn how to drive, Mr. Walny stood outside the car and had me look in my rearview mirror and my side view mirror, and as he walked along the passenger side of the car he showed me that there was a place where I could not see him through either mirror. It was my blind spot, and I know I always need to check it.

Every person has a blind spot. Think of it. When you are on the road, tons of metal, rubber, and plastic can be hurtling three feet from you going seventy miles an hour, and you can't see it. That's how big our blind spot can be, and it can be as big as a car.

Spiritually speaking, one of the hardest things to accept is that we have a blind spot. As we go about our daily lives, we carry with us a huge blind spot—a space in our life that when someone or something comes into it, we can't see it.

Great literature and mythology tell their stories of the great hero who carries with him or her the heroic or tragic flaw. Achilles is invincible from head to toe, left vulnerable only at his heel, and there he received the poison arrow from the bow of Paris, which falls the great warrior. Oedipus the king knows all things, except the one thing he most wants to know: the identity of his mother. King Lear has the world in his hand except that he does not know whom in his family he can trust, and he ends up trusting the wrong ones. Macbeth's quick rise to the throne is accompanied by the things he can't control: his fear and paranoia. All the stories speak to the fundamental truth of your existence and mine; we each have a blind spot—a place we can't see that leaves us vulnerable to tragedy, a sin that blinds us and makes us do the very thing we shouldn't do, or not do the very thing we should.

The Bible also carries with it the great stories of tragic flaw. Cain and Abel. Samson and Delilah. Paul and his thorn in the flesh. And, of course, the story of David. David, the king of Israel—not just a king, but a righteous king. A king whose heart was strong for God and a man who wished to please God, he seems to have it all—the kingdom of Israel, the favor of the people, the trust of his army, the love of his God. But there comes the day when he looks over the city and sees Bathsheba bathing, and he is undone. An affair ensues. Pregnancy follows. A cover-up is attempted. Murder is committed. Through all this soap-operatic, tragic drama, David still cannot see. He has a blind spot. He still thinks he is all the things he thinks he was. He still reads and believes his news clippings.

But then in walks Nathan, David's truth teller. Nathan sees David's blind spot, his Achilles heel. And Nathan tells David a story about a poor man and a rich man. The poor man raises in his family a little ewe lamb, the prized possession of his home. But when the rich man must entertain a guest in his own home, instead of taking one of his own flock to prepare the meal, he takes the one prized lamb of the poor man. David is enraged at the story and demands the justice of death to fall upon the rich man. With that, Nathan says the four fatal words, "You are the man." Nathan points to the king's blind spot and says, "You cannot see it, can you? You have this place in your life that is blind, it is as big as a Mack truck. No mirror can catch it. It is your undoing. It has allowed you to do very pathetic and tragic things."

No one wants to imagine that they carry around a blind spot. Even if we do imagine it, it's hard for us to see it—obviously. Blind spots arise out of our natural brokenness. They are defense mechanisms or false pretensions—things we do without knowing we do them.

For some it's about control. Your blind spot is that you don't think anyone can do it as well as you.

For some it's about low-self esteem. Your blind spot is that you feel like you always have to prove yourself to those who matter most to you.

For some it's about pride. Your view of yourself is a little too polished, and you'd hate to think that it has some tarnish.

For some it's about an old wound. You were wounded long ago, and the slings and arrows of rage and anger you cast upon those you love and don't love don't feel like such a big deal—except to those who have to absorb the slings and arrow of your rage and anger.

For some it's about ego. Your blind spot is that you really do think it's about you. You would hate to think that the universe does not spin on your axis.

The list goes on and on.

In 2 Samuel 12, Jesus is on the road again. We've heard the story about the men who were on the road to Jericho—three whose travels take them past the beaten man on the side of the road. One stops. One sees that the way of Christ is not as much about what is at the end of the road as what is alongside the road. God would have us pay attention to the present. Such is what happens on the road to Jericho.

But today Jesus is on the road going out of Jericho, and along the road he sees a blind man, Bartimaeus, who is blessed with a great yearning. He wants to see. He wants Jesus to change something fundamental about him. He knows enough about himself to know that he doesn't want to be what he is; he wants to be something more. He calls out to Jesus, "Have mercy on me."

One of the greatest steps in the spiritual journey is the step we take when we call out to Jesus—when we are blessed with a great yearning, when we recognize that we are the ones on the side of the road. We are not the ones who are there to help; we are the ones who are there to be helped. We have this blind spot, this Achilles heel that is exposed, this fatal flaw baked into our DNA—and we don't know what to do about it. Have mercy on me, Son of David! Jesus says, "What do you want me to do?" And the blind man says, "My teacher . . . my teacher . . . my teacher . . . let me see again."

How close are you to saying that? "My teacher, let me see again." Are you convinced that you see all that needs to be seen? Is your view of the world 20/20? Do you have everyone in your life figured out? Do you trust yourself so much that you can't imagine being the one on the side of the road, calling out to Jesus, "Have mercy on me!" Can you imagine a different and truer view of you than the one you see?

Like the man who had one drink too many, and he turns to his wife and says, "You know, I think you've been drinking too much. Your face is starting to get blurry."

Remember George Bailey in the movie *It's a Wonderful Life*? George has spent his whole life trying to take care of the little town he lives in—Bedford Falls. He's trying hard to protect the common citizens from the evil clutches of the rich and greedy and nasty Mr. Potter, but he grows discouraged, never seeming to catch a break. Finally he just can't see anymore. He can see with his eyes, but he can't see with his heart.

He can't see what a wonderful town he lives in and what a wonderful life he lives. His attempt to end it all is thwarted by an angel who shows him what the town would be like if he had never lived—the plight of his family, his wife, and his friends if he had never been around. Why, wicked old Mr. Potter took over the town without him there! Finally George Bailey sees. He sees something he couldn't see without help from the angel. He sees the beautiful town and the wonderful life. They'd been in his blind spot. He calls out to Clarence the angel and says, "Take me back. Take me back. I want to live again."

I was blind, but now I see.

They might be the most important days of our lives—those days when we intuit that what we are seeing is not all there is. Moreover, the image we have of ourselves is not the image others are seeing, and certainly not the image God is seeing. Maybe we can't see our pride or our possessiveness. Maybe we can't see our wound, our rage, or our anger. Maybe we can't see our ego. Maybe we can't see our desperate attempt to be loved. Maybe we can't see our bitterness or our two-facedness. And maybe the greatest moment of our lives is when we just call out, "Son of David, have mercy on me. I don't think I can see."

For fifteen years my office was on the floor above the community room of the church I served. Every Monday night at 7 p.m., fifty-two weeks out of the year, a group of twenty-five or thirty people gathered in that community room, and they were all there for the same reason. They all had the same blind spot; they were powerless in the face of alcohol. They were alcoholics. For many of them it was a blind spot that for years they didn't even know they had. Others knew it, but they didn't. Most of them had done pathetic and tragic things. But somehow, someway, for each of them, their eyes had been opened, and they could see what they hadn't before seen. And they were there every Monday night to remember again how badly they needed to keep checking their blind spot—how badly they needed to call upon a higher power, a power greater than themselves, to restore their sanity.

On the road out of Jericho walks the higher power, the greater power. Around him is the crowd. Maybe the wisest of those crowded around is the one on the side of the road, the one calling out to the power, calling out to the Son of David, "Have mercy on me. I want to see again."

"You are the man." "You are the woman." Would that we all could have a Nathan in our lives—if only to help us know that maybe the biggest step is still ahead, the step that says, "My teacher. My teacher. Have mercy. I am the blind man. I am the blind woman. There are things to see that I can't see. And I am powerless to even know what they are. My teacher, my teacher, let me see again."

ᏟHE ᏒIGHT ᏚTUFF

Genesis 1:1–13

SOMETIMES WE DON'T treat each other the way we are supposed to be treated.

Where I grew up, there was a girl named Julie Johnson; at least that is the name I'm giving her. Julie Johnson had a severe case of the cooties. No one knows quite how she got them, but someone, somewhere along the way at Gordon Elementary School diagnosed Julie Johnson with cooties. The reason, of course, is that Julie didn't look quite right. She was a little overweight. She walked sort of funny. She had a loud voice. She was socially awkward. That's about all you need for a diagnosis of cooties. And because this was long before the HIPPA requirements regarding privacy, everyone knew that Julie had this American elementary school equivalent of leprosy. The word was that Julie Johnson was so badly infected, not only were you not to go near her, you were not supposed to touch the ground anywhere near where she walked. Every morning on the Gordon Elementary playground, whenever anyone saw Julie approaching, that person would start to yell in a sort of chantlike cadence, "John-son, John-son." And as soon as you heard someone yell "John-son," you were supposed to start yelling it, too. Not only that, you were supposed to jump onto some piece of playground equipment so as to get your feet off the ground when Julie Johnson walked by. That's what we did every morning at Gordon Elementary: "John-son, John-son," as Julie Johnson with head bowed low would walk through our playground on her way to class while every one of us—on top of the jungle gym, the slide, the swing set, the chin-up bars—was escaping the infection of Julie Johnson.

Cruelty starts early, doesn't it? Something like that happens in just about every elementary school in America—and not just America but the world. Somebody is getting picked on, somebody is getting made fun of, somebody is getting ostracized.

Usually it's for no good reason—not that there could be any good reason for such treatment.

I told the story of Julie Johnson at a youth conference a few years ago, and when the service was over, a very attractive college coed came down and waited in line to talk to me. She said, "I'm Julie Johnson." She wasn't the Julie Johnson of Gordon Elementary, but she was the Julie Johnson of West Allis, Wisconsin.

"How could this be?" I asked.

"Oh," she said, "I once did not look like this."

When you stand in adulthood and look back upon such childhood shenanigans, you are left to scratch your head that such things could happen, but they happen long after childhood, too. Sociologists, psychologists, and anthropologists all have their theories on why we perpetrate such meanness. Social hierarchy, herd mentality, low self-esteem—the theories are endless. And yet you wonder if part of it might be that as children, and as adults, the reason we treat our fellow humans so inhumanely is that we just didn't read our Bibles.

Not long into the Bible—within the first two pages—we read something that speaks to fundamental human nature. The first chapter of the book of Genesis tells us that the universe coming into being didn't happen by accident. Endless are the scientific theories as to how the universe came into being, many of them very plausible and credible—the big bang perhaps the most widely held. The writer of Genesis would not seek to argue such points. But what the writer of Genesis would say is that no matter what theory you subscribe to, the universe did not come into being by accident. Someone lit the fuse for the big gang. Someone set the stars in the sky. Someone put the earth into orbit. Someone's spirit moved over the face of the deep. Someone divided the heavens from the earth. Someone made the beasts of the field. Some intelligent and wildly creative mind put this all into being.

One day I was out at Myakka State Park, the largest state park in Florida, and I was taking a tour around the lake. The guide was pointing out this and that bird, and this and that tree, and telling us about alligators and how they nest and hatch—and it doesn't take long before the evidence becomes incontrovertible that there had to be some mind, some design behind all of this—that each and every part of creation began as an idea in the mind of the Creator.

That is precisely what the Genesis writer wants to tell us. "In the beginning when God created the heavens and the earth . . ." It says something about the Julie Johnsons of this world, that in the beginning she was in the mind of God. Each of us was in the mind of God.

The Genesis writer also wants to make a point about the nature of the created order: When God thought us up, and when God put us into being, what was true about us from the very beginning was that we were good. God saw the light, and he saw that it was good. God saw the vegetated earth, and it was good. God saw the sun and the moon; they were good. God saw the wild animals and saw that they were good. God saw man and woman and saw that they were good, and God saw Julie Johnson and saw that she was good. God looked at everything he created and saw that it was very good!

When we were made, we were made from the right stuff, and within us we have the right stuff. Something is intrinsically good about you and me as God's creation. That's what Genesis wants to tell us.

I am the youngest of four boys. Two older brothers are pastors, and my third oldest brother is severely retarded. Jimmy is his name. He is four years older than me and lives in a state institution in Pennsylvania. He has never uttered a word. His cognitive ability is less than a four-year-old's. He does not know us as his brothers. He is now blind. People such as Jimmy, not too long ago, were treated very poorly. Inhumanely. Some would have made the case that creatures like Jimmy don't even deserve to live. But I read my Bible, and the Bible says on the first and second pages that whatever is created came out of the mind of God, and whatever is created God sees and he sees that it is good. Each and every one of us was, in God's mind, a good idea. Jimmy was a great idea. We see him differently, because we know that God sees him differently.

Do you know that about yourself? Do you know that you were a good idea of God? Please understand that I'm not here to excuse our part in fouling up what God has created. We have managed to bring brokenness upon ourselves. We have sinned and fallen short of the glory of God. It's the whole reason that Christ came—to pick up the pieces. But do you still realize that from the very beginning you were a good idea of God? This is the foundational and fundamental truth of who you are. You got your start because God had something great in mind. He still does.

Too many people—some here today—have managed to lose that sense of themselves. Despite what's happened, despite what we may have done to mar the image of God that has been imbedded in us, despite our willingness along the way to accept a less than divine purpose for our lives, each of us still has the right stuff: the mind of God and the image of God. When the apostle says, "In Christ we are a new creation," he is telling us that in Christ we are being brought back to that original moment when we were first created and God saw that it was good.

Can you see what God sees?

Do you see how life changes when we take ourselves back to the beginning? Do you see how life changes when we try to see creation as God sees creation? What might the world look like, what might the world be like, what might you look like, what might you be like if you and I were to put on the kingdom glasses—if you and I were to open our Bibles and see again how God sees the world?

Remember that haunting line in Arthur Miller's *Death of a Salesman* when the family of Willie Loman is standing at his grave? Willy Loman managed to live into his name—"Loman," low man. Always trying to land the deal. Always trying to make the quick buck. Always trying to realize the unrealizable dream. He dies a broken and tragic man. His wife, Linda, standing over the grave, says this in eulogy: "He never knew who he was."

Thank God we get to open our Bibles and read from the first words who we are. We are not an accident; we are the idea of God. We are not made of junk, but we are made out of the right stuff. We are the *imago dei*—the image of God—the imagining of God. We are the good imagining of God, given the chance in Christ to become the new creation.

The story about Julie Johnson has an ending. It happened when Mrs. Michaels died. Mrs. Michaels was a first-grade teacher at Gordon Elementary. She appeared to most of us to be as old as God, so we made fun of her, too—all of us except for Julie. Julie loved Mrs. Michaels. Julie would stay after school to help. She'd clean erasers and wash the chalkboard for Mrs. Michaels. Mrs. Michaels had been a member of my father's church, so my dad made me go with him to the funeral home to see Mr. Michaels. I didn't want to go, but I did. And when I got there, I kind of sat in a chair in the front of the room waiting for it to be over. All of a sudden, who should walk into the room but Julie Johnson?

"Oh, no," I said to myself, "what is she doing here?" I don't remember, but I might have even lifted my feet from the ground to avoid the cooties.

But then I watched as Julie made her way to the casket all by herself, and she went right for Mr. Michaels, and she grabbed him and hugged him, and in the midst of her tears she said to him, "I loved Mrs. Michaels very much." And Mr. Michaels hugged her back and said, "Well, Julie, she loved you very much, too. You were her special friend."

And then I knew. I knew that what the Bible said was true. Each and every one of us is a good idea of God. And in Christ, always a new creation.

$\mathscr{B}$ACKYARD $\mathscr{A}$DVENTURE

Acts 3:1–10

THE *NEW YORK Times* ran a report looking at the history of exploration over the last one thousand years and the status of exploration today. Certainly the last millennium has been filled with wonderful and enchanting adventures of the great explorers—Marco Polo to China, Columbus to the New World, Lewis and Clark through the Northwest United States, David Livingston to Africa, Darwin to the Galapagos Islands, and Neil Armstrong and Buzz Aldrin to the moon. The frontiers have been many in the last one thousand years. But now, as we enter the third millennium after Christ, the reality is that the world has been discovered. The earth has been completely mapped. There are no more frontiers. No more unclimbed mountains, no more uncrossed oceans to sail, no more uncharted jungles to traverse. The human race collectively is now in a time that when we look at every physical point in the world we can say, "Been there, done that." Someone comes down from Mount Everest—yeah, so what? Person flies across the Atlantic—what took you so long? Safari to Africa, the only shots are from your camera.

We've been here and there, we've done this and that, we've gotten the T-shirt— and now all the adventures we take are ones already taken. On the face of it, we appear to have nowhere else to go. Been there, done that.

It may be among the reasons that two words people most frequently use to describe their day-to-day condition are "busy" and "boring." Ask people *how* they are doing, and they will tell you, "Busy." Ask people *what* they are doing, and they will tell you, "Nothing."

"Hey, how ya doing?"

"I am so busy!"

"So, what you been up to?"

"Oh, nothing."

We are busy doing nothing? My guess is that when Lewis and Clark or Armstrong and Aldrin or Christopher Columbus got stopped on their way and asked how they were doing, they would have come up with something different than "busy," and they certainly would not have told you that they were doing "nothing."

When you become a culture that is busy doing nothing, it certainly explains why the word "adventure" has been replaced by the word "amusement." Our lives are no longer built around adventure, they are built around amusements. We live to be amused. When you are busy doing nothing, the only thing that keeps you from going insane or falling into despair are the amusements.

But is there not deep in the heart of the human soul a hunger for adventure?

British explorer Ernest Shackleton, in preparation for his expedition to the South Pole back in the year 1900, placed this advertisement in the London newspapers: "Men wanted for hazardous journey. Small wages, bitter cold, long months of complete darkness, constant danger, safe return doubtful. Honor and recognition in case of success." Shackleton said that the response to his ad was so overwhelming that it seemed that every man in Great Britain was determined to accompany him. People were dying for adventure!

Stephen Ambrose, in his great book on Meriwether Lewis and the Lewis and Clark expedition, quotes from Lewis's journal as he started into what he knew was going the most dangerous and uncertain journey of his life. Lewis wrote, "We are now about to penetrate a country at least two thousand miles in width, on which the foot of civilized man has never trodden; the good or evil it has in store for us is for experiment yet to be determined. I can esteem this moment of my departure as among the most happy of my life."

Is there not deep in the heart of the human soul a hunger for adventure?

And what does the world have to offer in response to this hunger? We get to go home and watch episodes of *Survivor* or *The Great Race* or *Swapping Nannies*. Is this our last frontier for adventure?

That's why I love the New Testament, and the Old Testament for that matter. The New Testament, the story of our genesis, is basically one long adventure story—not an *amusement* story, an *adventure* story. The story of Scripture is a story of people who have decided to pursue the uncharted lands and waters of the expanding kingdom of

God. It is a story of people whose lives have revolved around bringing the truth and grace of the gospel into the unknown regions of people's hearts. There has never been a more dangerous, exciting, thrilling, and adventurous task than when the church took up the commission to make disciples of all nations. Ours is a history of two thousand years of adventure. The two words "Christian adventure" are supposed to be redundant.

Today, however, they're not. Many in the church believe that the Christian faith is intended primarily to be an amusement; once you get your ticket into the park, once you take your seat in the pew, then your faith is intended to make you happy and peaceful and content and that's all.

But what about the great *adventure* of Christianity? For Christianity to become an adventure, it seems to need one thing, one essential ingredient, for you and I to take the risk of entering into the expanding frontiers of the kingdom of God. That one essential ingredient is a passionate belief that Christianity is true.

Arthur Compton, winner of the Nobel Prize in physics, said, "Every discovery I ever made, I gambled that the truth was there, and then I acted on it with faith until I could prove it true."

When we believe Christianity is true, we act on it in faith, and we find the proof of the truth in what we've been able to do through God's spirit.

I love the story of Peter and John going up to the temple. It is in the early days of the church and they are going up to pray. At the Beautiful Gate leading into temple is a lame man asking for alms. Probably there were dozens of people there asking for alms—people down on their luck. Peter passes by one man who has probably caught his attention, and there comes this moment. Call it a moment of truth. Peter asks himself, *Can Jesus Christ help this man? Do I believe that Jesus Christ can heal this man? If I don't believe it, then I walk on by and go into the temple and amuse myself with prayer, but if I do believe it—if I believe Jesus Christ can heal this man—then that is the first step into the adventure of faith.* Peter turns to the man and says, "Listen, I don't have what you're asking for, a little money, but what I do have is Jesus Christ, and in the name of Jesus Christ, get up and walk." Peter then held out his hand and helped the man to his feet. Something about that moment was very risky, very adventurous. Peter did not know for sure whether the man was going to be able to walk. But he did know Jesus, and he did know that Jesus could make him walk. That's why he held out his hand: because he believed passionately in the power of Jesus.

Adventurous Christians are people who believe passionately in the power of Jesus Christ. Adventurous churches are churches that believe passionately in the power of Jesus.

Do you know where the greatest adventure may lie for you and me? The greatest adventure may lie somewhere as close as your next-door neighbor, or the person down the street, or the kid who sits next to you in school. The greatest adventure may be rooted in whether we believe that Jesus Christ has the power to transform the lives of people we see every day, and then taking the huge risk of introducing Jesus Christ into those lives. The greatest adventure may be found when we believe in looking at the world's ills—and there are many—that Jesus Christ is the answer. He becomes the answer one life at a time. The adventure comes to us when we reach out our hand to the world and say, "In the name of Jesus Christ, walk."

And, man, that can be scary sometimes. But when did "scary" get dropped from the Christian vocabulary?

An elder in our church invited our family up to the Poconos to spend the weekend with his family. When we arrived I was informed that the first activity of the day for me was a biplane ride—one of those crop-dusting, open-cockpit, leather-cap-and-goggles-on-your-head kind of planes. "Who is going to give us this biplane ride?" I asked.

"Oh, some fellow down the road who has a sign out in his front yard that says he gives biplane rides."

"Do you know this man?"

"No, but it will be great—unless, of course, you don't feel up to it, Steve."

My male pride had now been challenged. Off we went to the man's house who gives biplane rides. To make a long story short, before I knew it, I was strapped tightly into the front seat of a biplane with my leather cap and goggles on, and behind me in the pilot's seat was a man who looked like the Red Baron, and who was just about as old as the Red Baron would be today.

The Red Baron proceeded to give me the flight plan. We would take off down the grass runway strip and fly up over the trees. We'd take a ride for a little while, and then he said that suddenly I would experience a sharp change in altitude. If I didn't like that sharp change in altitude, I should just raise my hand so he could see it, and he wouldn't do anything more like that. But if he didn't see my hand, he would do a few more things and bring us back to earth.

Off to the edge of the grass runway strip we went, and as we sat there waiting for takeoff, I said to myself, *What in heaven's name am I doing here? Sitting in a biplane being piloted by a man I have never met, who may not even have a pilot's license for all I know, a man who when we asked if there were insurance waivers to sign, said, "Nah. If you go down, I'm going down, too, and who are you going to sue?"*

Off we went, up over the trees and up toward a most spectacular view of northeastern Pennsylvania and the Pocono Mountains. Then came the sharp change in altitude. Straight down. When you are aimed straight down at the earth in a biplane piloted by the Red Baron, you have no thought of letting go one of your hands to wave it. No hand was seen waving, which was the Red Baron's signal to keep on going. So up we went next, straight toward the sun, and then completely over. After that, a couple of barrel rolls. And then back up to the sun, completely over again, and then straight down to the earth . . . but this time he cut the engine. With the propeller at a standstill and our plane plummeting to the earth, I thought to myself I wonder what tomorrow's newspaper would say: "Stupid Presbyterian pastor and Red Baron die during a stupid biplane ride."

Needless to say, the engine got going again, and the Red Baron soon landed us safely onto the grass strip alongside his house. Never have I been more glad to touch the soil, and never again have I spoken to my friend. (Just kidding.)

Am glad I took that ride? Yes. Why? Because I was alive, I was at the edge. And that was just an amusement! But still it felt risky, even dangerous, and in that risk and danger you really feel alive.

When Jesus Christ invites us into a real adventure, into the unknown regions of people's hearts, he invites us to come alive—to live on the edge.

When James Baker was secretary of state under George H. W. Bush, he developed a friendship with his Soviet counterpart, Eduard Shevardnaze. Through the pain and grief of his first wife's death, James Baker had become a Christian, and when his friend Shevardnaze had come to the United States on a diplomatic mission, it dawned on James Baker that while there may be diplomatic "answers" to the world's problems, there was really only one answer: Jesus Christ. So Baker invited Shevardnaze out to his ranch in Wyoming to go fishing. While the two men were out on the lake fishing, Baker decided to embark upon the greatest adventure of his life—something harder for him to do than bringing about world peace. He decided to share his faith in Jesus Christ with Eduard Shevardnaze. And so on a little boat in the middle of a Wyoming lake, James Baker embarked upon the wildest adventure of his life, introducing Jesus to one of the most important men in the world. Not long after that, Shevardnaze was back asking questions. Eventually he became a Christian. What huge risk! What an adventure! World politics in the balance—and still, a conversation about Jesus.

You and I are on this amazing adventure, an adventure into the unknowns of people's hearts. The woman next door whose marriage is starting to fall apart—does Jesus Christ have power for her life? The guy at work, the muckety-muck who's really unhappy underneath it all—does Jesus Christ have power for his life? The kid sitting next to you in history class who is prone to fits of violence and who is rumored to be making a bomb in his garage—does Jesus Christ have power for his life? The lonely senior citizen who wonders what the purpose of life is anymore—does Jesus Christ have power for his life? The welfare mother with four kids—does Jesus Christ have power for her life? These are the great adventures, my friends. They all begin with what we believe about the gospel.

"I am not ashamed of the gospel," wrote the apostle. "It is the power of God for salvation to everyone who has faith."

Wayne Gretzky, that great theologian, said, "I have missed every shot I didn't take." Make your life an adventure. Reach into the unknown regions of someone else's heart. Extend to them the hand of Christ. Help them to walk. For God's sake, help them to walk.

⟨𝒯⟩HROWING ⟨𝒴⟩OUR ⟨ℋ⟩AT IN THE ⟨ℛ⟩ING

Matthew 15:21–28

AN EPISCOPALIAN COLLEAGUE of mine told me the story of taking his ten-year-old son on a little father-son fishing trip. The two had been planning the trip for several months, and the boy was very excited about spending time with his dad and doing something they both loved—fishing. The boy packed and repacked his suitcase at least five times. They went shopping for the best fishing tackle. They charted out what streams and lakes they wanted to fish up in New England. By the time the day rolled around, the boy was almost beside himself. Having slept hardly a wink the night before, the boy was up at 6 a.m. knocking on his dad's door. They loaded up the car, said good-bye to Mom, and off they went. The trip of a lifetime.

On the second day of the drive up to New Hampshire, my friend got a call on his cell phone from the church secretary. Mr. Phillips, one of the pillars of the church, had died unexpectedly. The widow was beside herself. After a couple of calls, it became clear to the reverend that he had to go back. This was one of the pastoral moments he could not pass on to someone else. He got into the car and looked over to his son and told him the news. The trip was off. They would do it another time soon. My friend turned the car south and began the return home. In a little bit, the dad looked over at his son and could see big crocodile tears dripping down his cheeks.

"I'm sorry, Son. I really am," said the regretful father.

The boy responded, "It's not fair, Dad. It's just not fair."

We all know a little bit about what that boy was feeling. To some measure, life is not fair. Things happen that don't make sense. Bad things happen to good people. Cheaters win. Children suffer. The good die young. We know all the phrases, and in the midst of it all, questions arise: Where is God in all this? How can God let these things happen? How can a good God let evil exist?

A dear friend of mine from college was one of those people who seemed, at least to me, to embody what it meant to follow Jesus and live in the Spirit. She was a remarkable woman. After college she went to the mission field in Kenya and then to seminary and then to be a Presbyterian pastor. She was a humble saint who lived a simple life of love and joy, trust and faith. Anybody who knew her was drawn to her because they felt closer to God when they were in her presence. At the age of thirty she was diagnosed with cancer. She fought it and went into remission. She was diagnosed again. She fought it and went into remission again. She was diagnosed a third time. I felt bad the first time she was diagnosed, mad the second time, and indignant the third time. But when I got the call that dear, dear Janet had subsequently been killed in a terrible car accident, I hung up the phone and all those questions began to pour in. Why? How could God let this happen? What did she do to deserve this abandonment from God? It's not fair, God. It's just not fair.

But the question is, what do you do with those questions? What do you do when you have a bone to pick with God?

Golfer Tommy Bolt—a professional golfer playing in a PGA event—missed six straight putts. With the sixth miss he looked up toward heaven and said, "Okay, why don't you come down and fight like a man?" You've had those times.

We can imagine being in the shoes of the woman described in the reading today. She is the mother of a very sick child, a child possessed by a demon. That can mean a lot of things in the first century—but suffice it to say that the little girl is not well and her mother is beside herself. This is a Gentile family; they don't mingle with Jews. But the Jewish teacher/physician/miracle worker is in town. His name is Jesus, and this worried-sick mother doesn't care if he's a Jew. She only cares that her little girl is sick and maybe this man can make her well, so she goes to Jesus. She crosses the chasm of culture and religion, and she asks Jesus to make her little girl better.

We are used to stories like this in the gospel—someone needs healing, they go to Jesus, and Jesus immediately makes them better. Not so in this case. The woman jumps the chasm, lays her request before the rabbi, and Jesus says no, emphatically and hurtfully. "Let the children be fed first, for it is not fair to take the children's food and throw it to the dogs." In other words, "I have come for the people of Israel. I have not come for anyone else. There are the chosen ones and then there are the dogs." So much of Jesus's response we don't understand. We don't understand why he says no. We don't understand why he separates the Jews from the Gentiles. We don't understand why he feels the need to call this woman a dog. But he does.

It's not fair, Jesus. It's just not fair.

But this mother will not take no for an answer. She is not through with Jesus. She does not accept the status quo. She challenges Jesus. She throws her hat in the ring and invites Jesus to wrestle. "Okay, Jesus, you think I'm a dog. Well, even the dogs under the table eat the children's crumbs. I don't need to be anything more than what you think I am, Jesus. Call me a dog if you will, but just throw me a bone. Push a couple of crumbs off the end of the table. I just want my daughter well."

She's wrestling with Jesus. She's not giving up without a fight, and she is engaging, unbeknownst to her, in a very biblical exercise. She has thrown her hat in the ring, and she is wrestling with God.

She is harkening back to that time when Jacob—the scoundrel Jacob, whose conspiracy with his mother robbed his brother Esau of his birthright and blessing—has a wrestling match with God. It is a very mysterious story that takes place as Jacob is on his way to reconcile with his brother. He encounters a man in the night, and we are led to believe that this is no regular man; this is God, and God wrestles with Jacob through the night. God puts Jacob's hip out of joint, but Jacob will not let God go until God blesses him. Because this is who God is: God is the One who blesses. God is the One who heals. Jacob and the mother will not let God go until he heals and blesses.

It's the point of wrestling, you see. It's all through the pages of the Bible. We know the story of Job. Somewhere along the way Job got characterized as a patient man, and we were told to have the patience of Job. But Job was not patient! He wanted to wrestle with God. "My complaint is bitter," Job says. He continues,

> His hand is heavy despite my groaning. Oh, that I knew where I
> might find him, that I might come even to his dwelling! I would lay
> my case before him, and fill my mouth with arguments. I would

learn what he would answer me, and understand what he would say to me, there an upright person could reason with him, and I should be acquitted forever by my judge.

Job was not afraid to throw his hat in the ring and invite God into a wrestling match—to demand that God heal and bless.

The psalmist over and over again wrestles with the Almighty. "Why do you sleep, O Lord?" he asks. "Awake and do not reject us forever. Why do you hide your face and forget our affliction?" The psalmist demands healing and blessing.

Then there is Jesus in the Garden of Gethsemane: "Father, if it be possible let this cup pass from me." And on the cross: "My God, my God, why hast thou forsaken me?" Wrestling is going on between the Father and the Son. And all the Son wants is healing and blessing, and that is what he receives in the resurrection.

When the ways of God become far too mysterious to us, when the answers of God turn out not to be what we want them to be, when the events of life seem to indicate that God has checked out, we might be tempted to crawl away in resignation or defeat. We might even want to think that God was just a figment of our imagination. But we must not be afraid to be biblical. We must not fear to throw our hat in the ring. We must not step away from some wrestling with God—to demand healing and blessing—for this is who God is. It may not be the healing or blessing we were looking for, and it may end up that our hip gets out of joint—or that we are called a dog—but still we must demand that God be God and that healing and blessing come, and trust that it will be the healing and blessing God knows we need. We should never let God go until he blesses us.

The wrestling match began early for a young man named Henry Lyte. Henry was born on a farm in Scotland at the end of the eighteenth century. His father deserted the family when Henry was young. His mother packed him and his brother off to boarding school. At boarding school they got word that an illness had taken their mother's life along with their other brother's. That's reason enough to walk away from God. But Henry wrestled with his orphanhood. Henry was taken in by his headmaster and there learned more of God. He was called to the ministry and sought to serve the God with whom he'd wrestled. Henry became sick with various maladies, and he wrestled more. *Why me? Why must I get sick?* But still he served. He served several parishes until he settled in a little fishing village in Devon called

Lower Brixham. He served and wrestled there through more illnesses, including consumption. Finally Henry could go no further, and he retired from the parish. On his last Sunday he took a walk through the gardens and cemetery of the old parish chapel, watching the sun set. Moved by the scene and somehow changed by his wrestling with God, Henry Francis Lyte sat and wrote down the words that came to him:

> Abide with me.
> Fast falls the eventide;
> The darkness deepens;
> Lord, with me abide!
>
> When other helpers fail
> And comforts flee,
> Help of the helpless,
> O abide with me.

The wrestler had found his blessing. Two weeks later he died.

"It's not fair, Dad. It's just not fair," said the boy to his father. No truer words have ever been said. Too much happens in this world that we can't explain and that we don't understand. God seems painfully silent when sometimes we need him. But sometimes the only thing to do is throw your hat in the ring and invite God to wrestle with you. And never let God go, until he finally blesses and heals.

$\mathscr{P}$ OETRY IN $\mathscr{M}$ OTION

Psalm 105

OF ALL THE poems that Robert Frost ever wrote, the one he liked best is a simple two-stanza poem called "The Pasture":

> I'm going out to clean the pasture spring;
> I'll only stop to rake the leaves away
> (And wait to watch the water clear, I may)
> I sha'n't be long.—You come too.
>
> I'm going out to fetch the little calf
> That's standing by the mother. It's so young,
> It totters when she licks it with her tongue.
> I sha'n't be long.—You come too.

I'm not sure Frost ever explained why that short verse was his favorite, but if I were to guess, it may be that it's a poem that invites people to journey with him into his world of simple, natural beauty—an invitation to stop and observe for the moment all that is going on right in front of you, a world in which one stops to marvel in the simple chore of clearing a pasture spring or a newborn calf barely standing on four legs.

We live in a world of wonder. God is quietly moving all around us, and one of the great challenges of life is to see it, observe it, and wonder at it. For me, reading Robert Frost's poetry is a devotional experience because he invites me to do something that I don't often do on my own: stop and take inventory of God's movement and beauty going on right in front of me.

Who does not share the narrator's melancholy in the poem that we all likely read when we were young and in school, "Stopping by Woods on a Snowy Evening"? The traveler who stops to "watch the wood fill up with snow," and to hear and see the "sweep of easy wind and downy flake." Oh, "The woods are lovely, dark and deep, / but I have promises to keep, / and miles to go before I sleep, / and miles to go before I sleep."

We all have promises to keep, commitments to honor, meals to cook, games to watch, jobs to do, and miles to go before we sleep—and it's all at the great peril of missing the very beauty that rises and falls before us.

Maybe Jesus was addressing this problem when he pointed to a nearby meadow and said, "Consider the lilies of the field, how they grow; they neither toil nor spin, yet I tell you, even Solomon in all his glory was not clothed like one of these."

What debt we owe the poets and the prophets who see a world we don't often see, because we are too busy, too worried, too occupied, and with too many miles to go before we sleep.

Remember the Norman Rockwell painting of the busy city street with people walking to and fro—choosing not to look at each other, but all with their heads staring down at nothing except their own feet? But there stand the local rector and sexton posting the words and message for the sign that week: "Lift up thine eyes."

We all could stand the gentle reminders of the poets and painters and prophets to lift up thine eyes and see God's faithfulness.

Garrison Keillor might be calling us to such a reminder when he writes, "Faith rules through ordinary things: through cooking and small talk, through storytelling, holding hands, fishing, tending animals and sweet corn and flowers, through sports, music and books, raising kids, all the places where the gravy soaks in and grace shines through."

We open to the great poets of Scripture that we find in the book of Psalms—150 poems and prayers that invite people like you and me into a world that we often don't see: the world of God's faithfulness. Have you ever stopped to think what a debt of gratitude we owe to those people who wrote the 150 psalms? They not only experienced and remembered and felt the movement and faithfulness of God in their life and in the life of Israel, but thought to write verses about it. Can you imagine what our faith would have been like if the psalmists had not taken the inspiration of God and sat down and wrote words such as, "The Lord is my shepherd, I shall not want," or "God is our refuge and strength, a very present help in trouble," or "I lift up my eyes to the hills, from whence cometh my help"? It's all poetry, and it helps us to envision a world we often don't experience.

In Psalm 105 God invites the people of Israel into the world of God's faithfulness as found in their very own story. "Remember the wonderful works he has done, his miracles and the judgments he uttered," and if you were to read the entire 105th psalm, you would read the early story of Israel—God's faithfulness through the time of Abraham, Isaac, Jacob, and Moses. If you want to know about God's faithfulness, says the psalmist, look no further than our very own story. The poetry going on in the story of Israel points to the reality of God's faithfulness. "Right here," the psalmist says, "in our very own story."

What about our story or stories? Have you stopped to think of your own story as poetry in motion—that there might well be this wonderful script of God's faithfulness being written upon your days, and certainly upon the things that are taking place around you? Strange how you can be living in one world—the world of human events, human chores and errands and schedules and deadlines—and not see the world of God's faithfulness going on around you, within you, and over the course of your days. Life has a strange way of causing us to forget very quickly the story of God's faithfulness that has been unfolding in our own lives.

It's not unlike the story of the grandmother who was taking care of her grandson down at the shore. She got him all set up at the water's edge with his little bucket and shovel and hat, and she went to sit down in her beach chair. All of a sudden, a huge wave crashed onto the shore and swept the little boy right off the sand and into the sea. The grandmother saw all this and ran to the water's edge, and with a great feeling of helplessness she looked up to heaven and began to petition God: "Lord, you can't do this. This boy is barely a year old. You have to bring him back to me! Please give me my grandson back." Another huge wave came crashing to the shore, and with it came the little boy deposited in the exact same spot in which he had been sitting, shovel and bucket in his lap. The grandmother stared at the boy for a moment and then looked up to heaven and said, "You know, he had a hat."

Sometimes you can be living in the world of God's incredible faithfulness, poetry being written right upon your life, but you don't see it or remember it.

"Remember the wonderful works he has done, his miracles, and the judgments he uttered."

Is it possible that your life has been a succession of God's works and miracles? For some of you, the miracle has been survival. You have survived a tough life. The odds and circumstances were against you, but you did all right. For others the miracle is your faith. Despite the evidence and all the questions you have, you still believe. For some of you, the miracle is your family and friends; as much as you know about yourself you are astounded that people still love you. For others the miracle comes in looking back and seeing the near misses, the lucky breaks, and the chance meetings, and realizing that the explanation isn't coincidence, chance, luck, or even your own ingenuity. It was God all along.

So much of spirituality is a matter of looking back on your life and finding the thread of God's faithfulness that has woven together your days. When you locate that thread, you begin to discover that your life if the stuff of poetry. You are poetry in motion. Your life is the story of God's faithfulness. Your memories as you share them with your children and your children's children reflect the poetry of God's faithfulness.

I've said that I come from a family of pastors, four generations worth. Pastor families seldom get together for holidays, because on holidays we usually are in our pulpits. But every summer our families gather in North Carolina. Father, stepmother, brothers, wives and children, nieces, nephews, cousins. Four of us are Presbyterian ministers. We do it every year. Every night it's dinner together, and the conversation is mostly memories. Stories. We tell stories. Most of the stories we've heard a thousand times, but we keep telling them—maybe for our children's sake. Like most families the stories are a mixed bag: victory and success, mistakes and failure. We tell stories on ourselves about stupid things we've done or that others have done to us. We mostly laugh; we sometimes cry. But when we have the family prayer, we realize that, through it all—through all the stories combined and separate—the one constant has been God's faithfulness. God is the one who has brought us to this point. We are, in fact, his poetry in motion, God scripting the verse of his faithfulness upon our days. When we take the chance to stop and remember, how grateful we become.

Remember that old Gladys Knight and the Pips song where she sings, "If anyone should ever write my life story, / for whatever reason there might be. / You'll be there between each line of pain and glory, / 'cause you're the best thing that ever happened to me." I wonder, especially at a time like Thanksgiving, if that isn't a lyric we all could sing when we think back upon our lives and consider what God has done and is doing. If our lives are ever written about—or if we could pen a poem about our years—wouldn't we find God between every line of pain and glory? Our worship is simply to sing that refrain over and over again to God: "You're the best thing that ever happened to me."

WHEN DOES LIFE BEGIN?

Acts 2:1–13

I was out in California visiting a good friend of mine named Tim. Tim was pastoring a church north of Los Angeles in a little town called Port Hueneme, right on the Pacific Coast. While I was there Tim received an invitation from one of his parishioners for us to go sailing. I am not much of a sailor, but I grew up on a lake, so the idea of a little pleasure cruise on the Pacific Ocean sounded pretty good. Late that afternoon Tim and I made our way over to Bob's house. Behind Bob's house was this beautiful thirty-six-foot sailboat.

Four of us were going to take this little excursion on the Pacific, two of whom knew nothing about sailing. I was one of them. We got on the boat, checked some last-minute things, untied the lines from the dock, and off we went.

In order to get out to the ocean we had to pass through a series of canals and into a harbor and then finally out to sea. For a while we chugged under the power of the boat's motor to get us out to the ocean. Before we started out I hadn't realized how windy it was, and as we drew closer and closer to the ocean, the wind picked up more and more. All of a sudden, Captain Bob said, "Well, gentlemen, let's prepare to race." Race? Nobody said anything to me about racing. I thought this was a pleasure cruise—you know, nibble some cheese and crackers, stretch out, catch a tan. Before I knew it, the sails were up, the engine was off, the wind was blowing even harder, and the waves were getting wavier. I am, remember, not a sailor.

As we got out onto the ocean, the boat starting going this way and that way, giving new meaning to the phrase "keel over." The waves seemed to be tossing us around at their whim. Captain Bob was barking orders at us with a voice that betrayed a slight sense of panic, and it was all I could do to hold onto these lines which were holding the sails which were holding the wind which was driving us farther and farther from the shore. . . .

Then I began to think what a wonderful life I had lived.

We were on that ocean three hours, and it took me about the first half hour to realize we weren't going to die. We were well into the race—with the ocean spray in our face, and the wind whipping us around, and the boom going back and forth almost knocking my head off a few times—when I began to realize that this was not the end of my life; this was sailing. This happens when you put out into the deep, raise your sails, and let the wind take you.

I think of Pentecost, and I think of my sailing experience. Long ago, twelve men were huddled together somewhere in the city of Jerusalem, and they were waiting. They weren't quite sure what they were waiting for; Jesus had been raised from the dead and had ascended into heaven, and he had promised these twelve men that if they waited, something he called the Holy Spirit would come to them—and when the Holy Spirit came they would receive power.

So they waited. They waited. And they waited some more. And on a day called Pentecost—the fiftieth day after Passover—they were gathered together in one room, probably praying the prayers that good Jewish men pray on Pentecost, and the Holy Spirit came to them in the sound of the rush of a mighty wind. Because they had been waiting, because their sails had been lifted high into the sky, this wind—this Spirit—caught them, and the Spirit took them out onto the high seas. This Spirit took them out of that room and into the streets of Jerusalem, and beyond Jerusalem it took them across Palestine and into all the regions of the Roman Empire. They became witnesses, announcers of the good news . . . people who turned around the course of history.

It all began on a day called Pentecost. Today we call Pentecost the birthday of the church—the day when the church began to live. These men and this group were alive before, but Pentecost marks the time when they really began to live. You can live and then you can *really* live. Your heart can be beating and your lungs can be breathing, and you are alive. But then there is a different kind of alive: when you are living for a purpose and a reason, a life full of incredible meaning and power. Now that the Spirit had come, now that the wind had caught their sail, now that they had received power from on high, these men were really living.

You can live, you see, and then you can really live.

Ezekiel the prophet paints for us a picture of the valley of the dry bones. He paints this picture to show Israel—a people that had grown tired and weary in exile—that they don't have to live the dry and weary life. He tells them of another life—when the Spirit comes, when the breath of God blows upon them—and these dry bones come to life.

Are we living in the valley of the dry bones? We talk about working ourselves to the bone. We talk about being bone tired. Or we talk about being so busy that we feel like machines. Maybe we talk about being bored and unsure of why we are here. We are living, but are we really living?

Perhaps we have worked so hard at trying to achieve and accumulate those things that we thought were going to give us life, only to find that they don't give us life at all. Security and comfort and a position in the company . . . we work so hard tethering our boat to the dock and trying to keep it from rocking around too much, and then all of sudden we discover that we're really not sailing. We try so hard to control our own destinies that maybe we are afraid to let the sails go up, allowing the wind of God's spirit take us where he wants us to go.

Just because you're standing on a sailboat doesn't mean that you are sailing. Just because you're breathing and your heart is beating doesn't mean you're really living.

I was speaking at a youth conference, having lunch in the dining hall. I sat across from a high school student, a young woman, and I asked her what just about every adult thinks to ask a high school student: "What are you thinking about doing in the future?" I was prepared for the answer I was used to hearing: "Oh, go to college, find a job."

Imagine my surprise when she said, "I want to go to China and be a missionary."

I kind of choked and said, "Really?"

"Yeah," she said, "really. There's a whole nation—the largest in the world—and they don't know anything about how much God loves them. I want to change that."

I said, "Yeah, but what about the college thing, the job thing, the marriage thing, the career thing?"

"Life's too short," she said. "I want to do something in my life that I won't regret."

No cheese and crackers for this girl. Life was about putting up the sails, pushing off the dock, hitting the whitecaps. It's the life the Bible talks about—driven by the Holy Spirit, life with sails high in the sky full of the divine gales that take us to places we would never go on our own. The waves can get high sometimes, the boat can get pretty rocky, and it can feel like you are holding on for your dear life. But that's living, that's being on the edge, and that's the kind of life God created us to live.

Helen Keller—that great luminary born blind, deaf, and mute—was once asked to talk about the meaning of life. She said, "Life is a great adventure, or it is nothing at all."

In Philip Hallie's great book *Lest Innocent Blood Be Shed*, he tells the true story of a tiny French village in World War II that banded together to harbor Jewish refugees who were trying to escape the impending persecution of the Nazis. The village was led by a Protestant minister named Andre Trocme, who time and time again put his life on the line, as did so many others, to save the hundreds of Jews who came for refuge. Some forty years later, Hallie interviewed the children of these good French people who took such great risks to save their Jewish neighbors. As children, these people had experienced life-threatening conditions, given up their bedrooms and their food, had their houses full of strangers, and had the police search their houses week after week. When asked if they resented having to live this way, the children of that village—now adults—said that they would have had it no other way. It was the most thrilling time of their life.

When does life begin? For those of us who celebrate the day of Pentecost—who claim that the church's birthday is when the Holy Spirit came, that the church began when the wind blew—life begins when we dare to push off from the dock, raise our sails, and let the Spirit capture our lives and take us where God wants us to go.

So, my friend Tim—the one who was half responsible for getting me on the dumb sailboat a few years ago? I got a call from him late one night. "You know, Steve, I've been talking to a guy about becoming a missionary to Turkey."

I said, "Tim, Turkey? Turkey is 99 percent Muslim. They don't like Christians. They imprison missionaries. Turkey?"

He said, "Yeah, Turkey. I feel like God wants me to go out into the deep. I think God wants me to help bring Christ to Turkey." And that's where he went. He is teaching the young underground leaders of the Turkish church. He has cut his ties from the dock and set the sails, and he is living the life.

Oliver Wendell Holmes put it this way: "To reach the port of heaven we must sail, sometimes with the wind and sometimes against it—but we must sail, not drift or lie at anchor."

℘UTTING GOD IN ℋIS ℘LACE

Matthew 7:7–15

A LITTLE BOY was racing around the house while his mother was getting ready for dinner guests. He was making a mess here and making a mess there. His mom was always having to stop what she was doing to clean up something he had done, and she was just about at her limit. Then the little boy, rushing on his way out of the house, ran past the beautifully set dining room table, and his belt buckle caught hold of the lace tablecloth. Everything on the table flew off with an unceremonious crash.

The mother lost it. She chased her son out the door and watched him climb underneath the porch. She was just about ready to go in after him, but she realized that the guests would be coming soon. She decided to let her husband deal with it. When her husband came home, he heard all about what the boy did that day and the yanking of the tablecloth and how he'd better go out there and have a talk with his son.

The father went out and got down on his hands and knees and starting crawling under the porch. Way in the back he saw two little eyes staring at him. He kept crawling toward his son, and then he heard his little boy say, "Is she after you, too?"

Sometimes we can gain a reputation that is not quite deserved.

A study was done at Baylor University about what Americans believe about God. Thousands were surveyed and asked dozens of questions. The responses led the researchers to construct four general groups that Americans fall into regarding their understandings about the nature of God and how God fundamentally works. The folks at Baylor divided up believers in the United States—over 90 percent of the population—and placed them into one of these four categories:

- Thirty-one percent of Americans believe in what is called the *Authoritarian God*—a God who is deeply involved in our daily lives and world events, and who is angry at our sin and willing to punish the unfaithful.
- Twenty-four percent of Americans believe in what is called a *Distant God* who does not really interact much at all with our daily lives or with world events. He takes no pleasure nor holds any anger over what is going on in the world; he is more of a cosmic force that got the whole thing started and now sits back and watches.
- Twenty-three percent of Americans believe in what is called a *Benevolent God*— a God who is also deeply involved in our daily lives and world events, but largely as a positive force who is not eager to punish us.
- Sixteen percent of Americans believe in what is called a *Critical God* who does not really interact with our daily lives, but is still not very happy with how things are going in the world—and will at some point exact justice upon us.

This study didn't say much about how we came up with our ideas about God. Some across all four categories, I'm sure, would claim they get their view of God from the Bible. Others may have formed their ideas from parents or Sunday school teachers or friends or college professors or the latest book from Barnes and Noble. Along the way, though, God may have gained a reputation that is not much deserved. Our view of God may have something more to say about us than about God. If Mom was angry at the little boy, she must be angry at everybody.

Luke reports that the disciples came to Jesus and said, "Lord, teach us to pray." Learning how to pray straight from Jesus would obviously be an important lesson. What does Jesus say about how to address God? Who is this God whom we would come to in prayer?

"When you pray," Jesus says, "say, 'Our Father, who art in heaven, hallowed be thy name.'"

When Jesus shares with us this address to God, this image of God, he speaks out of his own relationship with God. Jesus invites us to pray "Our Father," because Jesus prays to God as Father. Jesus's conversations with God are born out of an intimacy between the Son and the Father.

So we look at those times when the Gospels give us an ear into Jesus's prayers, and we hear him pray "Father." Particularly in his passion—in the Garden of Gethsemane and faced with his time of trial—Jesus goes off on his own to be alone with his Father, and he prays, "Abba, Father." "Abba" is Aramaic for Daddy, or Papa. When he is trying to understand the will of the Father, Jesus calls him "Daddy." Like a little child looking for help and wisdom from the only place he knows he can get it. On the cross, as he is breathing his last, Jesus says "Father," *pater* in the Greek, "into your hands I commend my spirit." The Son knows that all he has left is the love and care of his Father in heaven. "I commend my spirit to my father," Jesus prays out of the personal relationship of the trinity. He is not praying to a man; he is praying into the personal dynamic and relationship of Father, Son, and Holy Spirit.

So Jesus in this gracious gift of the Lord's Prayer says, "When you pray, say, 'Our Father . . .'" In other words, "I extend to you the intimacy of the relationship the Son has with the Father. You can call him 'Father,' because that's what he is. He is your Father. And he is not only your Father, he is the Father of all. So don't pray 'My Father,' pray 'Our Father.' Pray not with just yourself in mind, but pray with everyone in mind. Pray as a member of the family of God's children, who would want the best not just for myself but for all those for whom God is Father. Lord, we pray to you together, and we receive from you together."

When I pray "Our Father," I pray listening to what my brothers and sisters are praying. I pray listening to what the guy next to me is praying. I pray listening to what my sister in Kenya is praying. I pray listening to what the child in Honduras is praying. I pray with them, to Our Father. And I receive with them, from Our Father.

"Our Father who art in heaven." This Father is as intimate as he chooses to be with his children, and yet is separate from them. He is our Father, and yet he is in heaven. He is separate from us, not a part of us. This truly is a relationship of two independent characters. God is who God is, not what I want him to be. God is not a characterization that a majority of Americans or anyone else makes him out to be. God is God. And most of that we don't understand, because God is in God's heaven, and God's ways are not our ways, and God's thoughts are not our thoughts. God is in heaven. He is not American. He is not Egyptian. He is not British. He is not Iranian. And as soon as we might try to make God conform to some particular government or denomination or party, that's about the time when we find ourselves in the biggest trouble. Because Our Father is in heaven.

And holy is his name. It is not just that God is in heaven, but our Father is holy. Our Father—though separate from us—yearns for intimacy with us and is nevertheless holy. God is the mysterium tremendum—the one who invokes fear and trembling. When Isaiah sees the Lord high and lifted up, his train filling the temple, Isaiah says, "Woe is me! I am lost, for I am a man of unclean lips." He's overwhelmed by holiness. The house fills with smoke. The pivots of the thresholds shake. Soon we realize that when Jesus teaches us to pray, he invites us into a relationship that is far beyond what we can figure out. God is personal, but he is not just my personal; he is our personal. God is concerned with the whole family, yet God is apart from the family. He is the Father in heaven. He sees what we cannot see. He knows what we cannot know. He loves in a way we cannot love.

Maybe that's some of what Jesus is trying to say in that great story of the Loving Father and the Prodigal Son. When the boy is let go to live life on his own terms and discovers in the pigpen how well that has worked out for him, and he comes to himself and goes back to the Father, the punch line is when the father runs to him. The standard line is for the son to grovel, working hard to earn the father's good graces. But the punch line is that the father runs to the son, welcoming him. The elder son comes in from the field, saying to the father, "I thought you were my father, not our father. I thought I was now your only son. I thought your love went only as far as the family compound." And the F/father says, "Surprise! You never know how far my fatherhood will go."

Condoleezza Rice, when she was provost at Stanford University, made a dash once into the supermarket to buy some things. In the produce section a woman engaged her in a moment of polite conversation and was prompted to ask Ms. Rice if she knew how to play the piano. Condoleezza Rice was an accomplished concert pianist, and so she said she knew how to play a little. "Could you," the woman asked, "play at our church?" Condoleezza Rice had been raised in the church, but her academic career led her away from it for a long time. For that reason perhaps, she agreed and ended up playing old gospel tunes for an African American congregation. She called her mother and said, "Mom, I don't play gospel, I play Brahms!" And her mother said, "Don't worry, just play in C, and they'll come back to you!"

When thinking about how this all got started in a supermarket produce section, Condoleezza Rice said, "God must have a far reach."

Isn't that what Jesus is pointing to in his early teaching in the Lord's Prayer? The Holy God of Heaven—Our Father who art in heaven, hallowed be thy name—this God of heaven has a far reach. As separate and as holy as God might be, his reach is even further.

You've heard a thousand times the likely apocryphal story about the great pianist Paderewski. He was on tour, and one night as a European concert hall filled with great expectation for the great master to enter the hall, a little boy escaped his mother, ran onto the stage, jumped onto the piano bench, and began to play his rendition of "Twinkle, Twinkle Little Star." The hall filled with anxious laughter, but before the mother could get to her son, the great Paderewski slowly walked onto the stage and approached the novice pianist. He leaned over—reaching to one side and the other with his left arm and right arm—and whispered into the boy's ear, "Keep playing." As the boy played the simple tune, the great Paderewski added to the staggered notes his own improvised harmony—and the two for a moment made marvelous music together.

God does have a far reach. His holiness encompasses our staggering lives, to make something out of nothing—this holy one of heaven come down to earth.

Maybe this little girl had it right: the daughter of a Yale professor who, when she knelt beside her bed for her nightly prayers, was heard to say, "Our Father, who art in New Haven, how did you know my name?"

Could it be true? That the one in heaven whose holiness shakes the pivots is the one we can call Father, *our* Father—whose reach is as far as we will take ourselves? And that as holy as his name might be, the mysterium tremendum is that he knows our name as well?

𝒴OUR ℳOVE

John 3: 1-10

JOHN 3 UNVEILS two of the most remembered sayings of Jesus— two sayings that just about every Christian and anybody else who has been exposed to Christianity could say that they have heard. The first one is, "No one can see the kingdom of heaven without have been born again." The translation from which I read actually says "born from above," likely a more accurate reading of the Greek. The second saying of Jesus we find in this encounter is John 3:16: "For God so loved the world that he gave his only Son, so that everyone who believes in him may not perish but may have eternal life." Two of the significant truths of the gospel are revealed in this one encounter with Nicodemus. Quite a conversation.

Some years ago I had the chance and the honor to see *Inherit the Wind* during a short revival run on Broadway. The play, as many of you know, is based on the Scopes monkey trial in 1928, which pitted two old rivals and friends, Clarence Darrow and Williams Jennings Bryan, against each other. In this particular production the two lead roles were played by none other than Charles Durning and George C. Scott. The trial is a battle over evolution and whether it should be taught in schools. When the trial is over and Bryan has won, the two lawyers are left on stage for a moment. Bryan laments to his old friend about how they have grown so far apart. Darrow has this intriguing rejoinder: "All motion is relative. Perhaps it is you who has moved away by standing still."

As we get on in years—and no matter what age we are, we are all getting on in years—"standing still" is an increasingly attractive posture, sometimes for good reason. When we get on in years, we discover some basic truths about life and faith and experience that lead us to stand firmly upon truths and postulates that we feel are nonnegotiable—deeply held convictions from which we are not willing to budge.

Other times we like the idea of standing still because, regardless of how wise it is to keep moving, it is more comfortable to just stay put. The older the dog, the harder to teach it new tricks. Ever since we were young, the pressure has been on us to get settled. To get established. To ensconce ourselves. To position ourselves. When you have dedicated your life to such things, budging becomes difficult. It is too inconvenient, too hard, too uncomfortable. We get set in our ways, yet that isn't always a good thing.

Sometimes pride is at stake. Maybe you have been living your life in a certain way, and facing that you got all or a part of it wrong can be rather painful. Turning back is hard once you've been down the road aways.

In Merle Miller's biography of Lyndon Johnson, the U.S. president who presided over America's deepening involvement in the Vietnam War in 1969, Johnson took time to reflect upon his handling of the crisis: "I never felt I had the luxury of reexamining my basic assumption. Once the decision to commit military force was made, all our energies were turned to vindicating that choice and finding a way somehow to make it work."

What a tragedy! Regardless of your opinion on that war, what a tragedy to get to a point where you cannot allow yourself the luxury of reexamining your basic assumption. So committed are you to where you have settled that you might not allow yourself the chance to consider a new way, a new idea.

I love the story about Nicodemus. If there was a man who felt he had the right to stay put, if there was a person who felt that it was too inconvenient to consider another way of looking at things, if there was a person who could have been convinced that he held the time-tested truth—it was Nicodemus. John tells us that he was a Pharisee, a leader of the Jews. He had settled right up there in the top ranks of his profession. He had a lot to lose by not standing still.

But what does Nicodemus do? He moves from the comforts of his home, from the security of his seat on the Sanhedrin, under cover of night. He makes his way over to where Jesus is. A clandestine rendezvous, perhaps. A meeting with this "teacher sent from God," as he describes him. With this movement comes an indication that Nicodemus had opened the door ever so slightly to the possibility of reexamining his basic assumption. He had seen Jesus perform his many signs and had realized that there had to be something special about him. Even though Nicodemus could not imagine that God had anything new to reveal to the world beyond the law and the prophets, Nicodemus moved over to talk to Jesus just in case his basic assumption wasn't right.

The amazing conversation Nicodemus ends up having with Jesus is one that could very well not have happened, but it took a person who was willing to open himself up to a fresh conversation. He had a lot to lose. Let us then not have the point be lost on us: no matter what position we have taken in our lives, no matter where we have settled, no matter how firmly established we are, no matter how well on in years we are, movement can be a good thing. It is never too late to reexamine a basic assumption.

We have basic assumptions about many things: career, lifestyle, time management, you're a reading of the Bible, retirement, other people. But it is never too late to reexamine a basic assumption, to have a fresh conversation with Jesus.

In Nicodemus's fresh conversation with Jesus, Nicodemus heard Jesus talk about being born again from above in order to see the kingdom of heaven. To that comment Nicodemus asks a very important question: "How can anyone be born after having grown old?" And while Nicodemus is suffering a little from extreme literalism here, his query has a deeper point: What chance does a person have to start over?

Nicodemus might have said, "Jesus, I have moved over to have a conversation with you. I have left myself open to a new teaching. I have allowed myself the luxury of reexamining my basic assumption, and now you are telling me that there is a chance that I will need to start over, be born from above? What chance of this is there? I'm a little set in my ways, you see. I'm an old dog that doesn't take kindly to new tricks. I'm on in years. How is this to be?" Good questions.

In response and in a nutshell, Jesus tells Nicodemus that his being born from above is a matter of surrendering to the movement of God's Spirit that is like the blowing of the wind. And when the wind blows, you can choose to do one of two things: you can spend all your energy and time trying hard to stand still, to stay fixed, to remain unmovable, or you can throw up your sail and let the wind, the Spirit, take you. And when you let the wind of the Spirit take you, all of a sudden you are living life in a different way. You're not stuck in the sand anymore. God is taking you to do and to believe and to experience things that you never thought likely.

Lauren Winner, in her great book *Girl Meets God*, tells of being raised Jewish and converting to the deeper discipline of Orthodox Judaism when she was in college. It was a spiritual practice in which she found great peace and comfort. She was a strict adherent to Orthodox Jewish practice, but then one night came a vivid dream about being rescued by a nameless man. It takes too long to describe all the facets of the dream, but suffice it to say that when she wakes, she wonders if the man might be Jesus. She doesn't know why she thinks that. After all, what business does an Orthodox Jewish girl have in wondering that Jesus is trying to deliver her through a dream? She asks several people about it, who refuse to entertain the possibility that Jesus might be trying to play a role in her life. Finally one of her friends said that, yes, as she described the dream, perhaps the person in the dream might be Jesus. And then she said, "But I didn't know that you would be open to seeing Jesus in your dreams. You're an Orthodox Jew, after all. An Orthodox Jewish life might not have very much room for Jesus."

Lauren Winner tried to put the dream away for two more years, but it kept coming back. Then, like Nicodemus, she moved. She wondered if God was up to something. She reconsidered her basic assumption, and she opened the New Testament and began a conversation with the Rabbi, the Teacher. She became born of the wind and the Spirit.

I don't know where you are in life. You might have things all figured out. You might have all the answers. You might think that all the truth can be found in the *Wall Street Journal* or the *New York Times*. You might be so religious that Jesus has nothing new to say to you. You might be so vain that you probably think this sermon is not about you (apologies to Carly Simon), or maybe something deep inside wonders if life holds more than what you have or where you are. You might be wondering if you have reached the point of no return. You might be wanting to ask the dumb question, "How can anyone be born after having grown old?" You might be afraid to open yourself up to a new teaching—afraid of how it might change things for you.

But what if—no matter who you are, whether by cover of night or in broad daylight—you took the chance to have a conversation with Jesus of Nazareth—a new conversation? What if you were to leave your life opened enough that you could hear a new voice, a new teaching from the one called Messiah? Maybe the voice will come from one of the Gospels in the New Testament, or from joining a Bible Study or talking to a pastor, or maybe talking to an elder to explore how you might start or restart your conversation with Jesus.

Sometimes God seems far away because we are the ones who have been standing still.

"Now there was a Pharisee named Nicodemus, a leader of the Jews. He came to Jesus by night."

No more standing still. Your move.

ᏟHE ᏀOOD ᎠEED

John 9:1–41

NO GOOD DEED goes unpunished.

Remember the name Richard Jewell? Back in 1996 Richard Jewell was the security guard at the Atlanta Olympics who noticed an unattended backpack underneath a park bench in the middle of the Olympic Plaza and suspected that it might be a bomb. At the risk of being branded as an overzealous and hyper-paranoid security freak, Richard Jewell went to work right away warning people that there might be a bomb and trying to usher them away. Sure enough, his suspicions were right. The bomb exploded thirteen minutes later, tragically killing one person and wounding at least a hundred others. The results could have been much, much worse had Richard Jewell not been alert and risked himself to save others.

Immediately he was branded a hero—his alertness and courage having saved so many. But soon after, law enforcement officials began working on a theory that perhaps Richard Jewell was not a hero but someone who instead wanted to create a crisis in order to make himself a hero. Before he knew it he was listed as a possible suspect in the case. His listing as a suspect was leaked to the press, and within minutes a trial by media commenced. Soon the world had convicted the hero and made him the villain. He was called names. Reporters and photographers invaded his property. Those who once believed him, doubted him.

It took weeks to determine that Richard Jewell was not a suspect, but a hero. It took nine years to completely exonerate him, when the real culprit, abortion clinic bomber Eric Robert Rudolph, was arrested. Richard Jewell died two years later from a bad heart, some say a broken heart.

No good deed goes unpunished.

With that extrabiblical proverb in mind, we look at the middle of the Gospel of John and find something very interesting. John 9 relates the wonderful story of a man who was blind from birth receiving his sight from Jesus—a moment for celebration, one would think, but instead it becomes a moment of interrogation. Those in control of the temple and synagogue don't like the fact that this rogue rabbi is starting to get headlines, and they can't believe he has the power that people say he has. They launch an investigation: How could Jesus do these things?

Not only that, but Jesus begins speaking in terms that make a lot of people uncomfortable. He begins to suggest that he is not just a rogue rabbi but that he has a special relationship to God. "I am the gate," he says. "I am the good shepherd," suggesting that he is not just a rabbi, but *the* rabbi. And not just *the* rabbi—but maybe, just maybe, the Messiah. This situation prompts the question from the temple leaders: "How long," the temple leaders ask. "How long will you keep us in suspense? If you are the Messiah, tell us plainly."

We want the truth, they say. Remember the courtroom scene in *A Few Good Men* where Jack Nicholson, playing the rogue colonel, is interrogated by the JAG officer? "I want the truth." Nicholson shouts back, "You want the truth? You can't handle the truth."

We want the truth, they say to Jesus. Jesus basically tells them they can't handle the truth, because the truth, Jesus says, "is that the Father and I are one." *Yes, I am Messiah. You want the truth, I am the truth.* Having heard Jesus's assertion, those who can't bring themselves to believe "took up stones to stone him."

No good deed goes unpunished. Heal a blind man one day, and the next day they're lining up to stone you.

But if someone asks for the truth, that's the kind of thing that can happen. You can get in a lot of trouble if you answer honestly someone's quest for truth. "Tell me the truth, what do you think about the president?" "What do you think about the governor?" "How about the tie I'm wearing?" "Do you like my hair?" "Does this dress make me look fat?" You can put yourself in a lot of danger trying to answer those kinds of questions.

"Tell us the truth, Jesus." And Jesus doesn't lay it out relatively. He doesn't say, "This is the truth as I see it." He simply says, "This is the truth. It is the truth for me and it is the truth for you." No one likes to hear the truth when it is positioned as the truth for them. "The Father and I are one. That's the truth."

C. S. Lewis put it this way:

[I wish] to prevent anyone saying the really foolish thing that people often say about Jesus: 'I am ready to accept Jesus as a great moral teacher, but I don't accept His claim to be God." That is the one thing we must not say. A man who was merely a man and said the sort of things Jesus said would not be a great moral teacher. He would either be a lunatic—on a level with the man who says he is a poached egg—or else he would be the Devil of Hell. You must make your choice. Either this man was, and is, the Son of God: or else a madman or something worse. You can shut Him up for a fool, you can spit at Him and kill Him as a demon; or you can fall at His feet and call him Lord and God. But let us not come with any patronizing nonsense about His being a great human teacher. He has not left that open to us. He did not intend to.

So Jesus brings with him a choice. This is who I am, this is the truth. Do what you want with it, but this is the truth. The leaders of the temple do exactly what they want with this information. They line up to stone Jesus.

No good deed goes unpunished.

And what is so good about the deed is not only that Jesus is Messiah, not only that the Messiah brings a power to heal blind men, not only that Jesus enfleshes God for us, but that the Messiah brings such a good promise: God through his Messiah is reaching into the world to hold onto us, and to never let us go. That's the mission of the Messiah, to grip us. "I give them eternal life," he says, "and they will never perish. No one will snatch them out of my hand, and no one can snatch them out of the Father's hand." The good news of the truth, or the truth of the good news, is that Jesus is here to say that he and the Father are one, and that the reason God in Christ is here is to grab hold of us and never let us go.

Is there any greater news? For people who have been delivered into a world filled with bumps and bruises, ups and downs, lions and tigers and bears; who have to scratch out a living; who must deal with all the uncertainties of life . . . isn't it good news to know that God in Christ has reached into the world and has grabbed hold of us and promises never to let go?

We have in our house a West Highland white terrier. Her name is Lexie, and she is a great dog. I can almost set my watch by the moment when Lexie comes to me at night—around 9:00—jumping onto the couch and holding in her jowls a little stuffed toy, usually a squirrel. She looks at me, and she is there to prove to me that she is not going to let this squirrel go. She wants me to grab an end of the squirrel and try to pull it out of her mouth. Every night she proves that she will never let go. I shake and I pull and I pick her up off the ground and twirl her around, and she doesn't let go. Lexie lives to prove that she will not let go. Above all things, not letting go gives her joy.

And I can't help but think that when God comes to us in Christ, it is to reveal God's greatest joy. Because God's greatest joy, I imagine, is showing us that he will not let us go. "No one," Jesus says, "can snatch you out of the Father's hand."

It's the whole point of the cross and resurrection: God reaching into the world, and despite the pain and the hurt and the stoning and the nailing, God's greatest joy is showing that he will never let go.

It would be like walking with a friend down a path, and what you don't know is that ahead of you is a precipice. You walk with your friend, and before you know it you are walking right off this cliff. Your friend grabs your arm as you fall, and you are left there dangling over the edge . . . but your friend promises that he is never going to let go, no matter how hard it might be to hold on. Now, the comfort you take in that promise is relative only to how much you believe that it's true.

On your friend's end of the grip, there's no greater joy than the fact that as you were falling, he caught you and now is never going to let you go. As much as it might hurt to hold on, his greatest joy is the fact that he is holding on. And that's what God does: he hurts to hold onto us, but despite the hurt, God's joy is in the grip. And that's where our salvation is: in the holding on.

The cross tells us that it hurts God to hold onto us—because we have this way of biting the hand that holds us.

An old story from India is told of a man who was sitting under an ancient tree whose giant roots meandered down into a swamp. While he sat there he heard a noise where one of the roots entered into the water. The man looked closely and could see that a scorpion had become helplessly entangled in the roots. He stood up from where he was sitting and balanced himself along the root where the scorpion was trapped. He reached down to try to pull it free, but each time he reached down to grab the scorpion, the scorpion would lash him with its tail, stinging him painfully. But the man kept trying, and each time he would get lashed with the tail. Finally his hand had swelled so greatly that he could not close his fingers, so he withdrew to the shade of the tree to wait for the swelling to go down. As he arrived at the base of the tree, he saw a young man up on the road laughing at him.

"You foolish old man," said the young man, "wasting your time trying to help a scorpion that can only do you harm."

The old man replied, "Simply because it is the nature of the scorpion to sting, should I change my nature, which is to save?"

And isn't that the truth of it all, the truth that sometimes we can't handle? In Christ—in the one particular person named Jesus of Nazareth—God has made his reach to grab us, we who walk amid the dangers of this world. And despite biting and stoning and nailing the hand that holds us, despite the good deed that does not go unpunished, God promises that he will never let us go.

It is God's greatest joy. And our only salvation.

$\mathcal{L}$ONG-$\mathcal{T}$ERM $\mathcal{I}$NVESTMENT $\mathcal{S}$TRATEGY

Matthew 25:14–30

PERHAPS ONE OF the most familiar and greatest pieces of symphonic music is Beethoven's Ninth Symphony, which starts out with that great sequence of notes: *dun, dun, dun, duuuuuh—dun, dun, dun, duuuuuh.* We've all heard it in one form or another. It is unforgettable. I read this week a description of the symphony that one person offered. She said,

> I could distinguish accurately between the cornet and the roll of the drum, the deep tone of the cellos and the singing of the violins, and as the human voice ascended, piercing the waves of harmony, I recognized it immediately. I heard the chord swell in exultation, becoming ever more ecstatic and flaring up boldly like a flame, and my heart stood still. The female voices seemed to me like an incarnation of a choir of angels as they streamed away in a harmonious flood of the purest beauty. Then the instruments and voices broke out together—an ocean of wild oscillations—and died away like the breath of the mouth, vanishing in sweet softness.

That's quite a description. If it were me I would be back at those first notes saying, "Boy, that sounds pretty neat." Imagine how humbling to know that the description I just offered came from none other than Helen Keller. Totally deaf Helen Keller listening to this great music, kneeling down in her home with the cover of the speaker off and with her hand on the membrane receiving the vibrations. This is how she heard the symphony—composed by Ludwig van Beethoven who, of course, was deaf when he composed it and deaf when it was first performed.

When I first came upon that story of Helen Keller—imagining that living room, picturing her kneeling next to the speaker with her hand upon the vibrating membrane, hearing things likely that I couldn't hear today with my full hearing—it made me wonder how I would have been in that same room sharing the inability to hear through my eardrums. Would I have found another way of listening and employed my sense of touch, risking the awkwardness that others would feel to see me crouched next to the speaker? Or would I have sat back and chose not to listen at all, resenting the fact that the other people in the room could hear and I could not? Would I have grown jealous over the fact that some people had gifts that I was never given?

This question opens up for me a bigger issue: How do I look at my own life, and how do I view the gifts I have and don't have? To be human is to be susceptible to viewing life in relative terms. I am who I am, relative to those around me. The value of my gifts is found in relationship to the value of other gifts around me. The abundance of my gifts is determined by the abundance of gifts around me.

A man was the piccolo player in his country's national orchestra, and one night the king was in attendance for the performance. The orchestra played the best it had ever played. The piccolo piece was played to perfection. The king was overwhelmed at what he heard, and when the performance was over, he stood up and said, "This concert was so beautiful that I owe you an enormous debt of gratitude. In fact, what I will do to show my appreciation is that I will fill each of your instruments with gold from my treasury." "There I stood," said the man in the back row, "with my piccolo."

It doesn't take much to view our lives in relative terms, and to be quickly discouraged by what we don't have.

Maybe that is the question at hand in Jesus' great story of the Servants and their Talents. I've mentioned that Matthew 25 contains three compelling stories of Jesus—all of which have to do with the return of Christ. One of those stories is about three servants whom their master has given talents to oversee while the master is gone. Talents were a lot of money. In today's economy, one talent would be worth about $750,000. One servant is given five talents, another servant is given two talents, and the third servant is given one talent. None of them are given instructions of what to do with the talents: just take care of them. The five-talent guy invests the five talents and makes five talents more (nice guy to know in today's economy). The second servant invests the two talents and makes two talents more. The third servant goes conservative, putting his one talent under his mattress, which in certain times isn't a bad place.

If you go to the economics department of the local college, you'll find divergent interpretations of this great story. The question would revolve around investment strategy, what's best to do in the long term and what's best to do in the short term. How do you get the biggest bang for your buck? Two in the story go aggressive, one goes conservative, and each reaps what he sows. But that's not, of course, what the story is about.

The story is about how the master views the gifts he has given. Basically, they are his, and they are to be invested with risk.

Frankly, that's not the way I typically look at my life nor my gifts. Whatever gifts I have—which are few, I'm kind of a one-talent guy—I often think as *my* gifts. I know God has given them to me, but now that I have them, they're mine—to hold, to spend, to invest, and possibly to lose. And because I see them as my gifts, I apply my own investment strategy to them. I go conservative; I go safe. I employ little risk. I hold back. I go for the mattress. But that's not the point of the story. The accounting—the point of our stories—comes when the master views the gifts he has given us. When that time comes, the returning Messiah will say, "What did you do with my gifts? How did you invest my gifts? What risk did you apply to my gifts?

Answering those questions to the Messiah can be a scary notion to consider, until we realize something important about this idea of gifts. The word in the Bible for "gift" is the Greek word *charis*, which is the same as the Greek word for "grace." On top of that, *charis* is also the word for "joy." Gift, grace, and joy . . . interconnected and inseparable. With these three concepts comes an important investment equation: Our deepest joy is found when we see the gifts of our lives not as our own but as grace given us by the master, and in seeing our gifts as grace, we are freed to invest them with risk. The investing itself brings the joy!

That's the view of the master. It's not the return nor the amount of gifts that mattered; it was the investing. Those who did the investing heard clearly, "Enter into the joy of your master!"

Some of you may know about Andrea Jaeger—a tennis phenom some decades back. At the age of fourteen she had entered the top echelon of professional tennis—during the era of Billie Jean King, Chris Evert, and Martina Navratilova—at one point becoming the number-two player in the world. She played in the finals at Wimbledon at age eighteen. Pretty heady stuff. But she was also desperately lonely. Shunned by her fellow professionals for being too young, and shunned by her classmates for being too good, one day out of sheer loneliness she went out and bought a bunch of toys and took them to a nearby hospital. She entered the pediatric ward and started handing them out to sick kids. Suddenly there came the rush of joy.

> They made me feel like Santa Claus. I went to give them something, and I ended up with the gift. There was this boy with stubs for hands who wanted to play video games with me and a girl who danced with her IV pole and a girl who asked me to rub her bald head. She was going through chemo and I thought, *When I grow up I am going to spend my life helping these kids.*

Grew up is what she did. She gave up tennis early due to a bad shoulder and began the Silver Lining Ranch—a camp for kids battling cancer. She started it first by burning through all her prize money, and then she started giving tennis lessons in exchange for donations—even working as a ticket agent at the local airport so that she could buy the kids discounted fares to get to the camp. Many of the kids who came to her camp didn't live long after. Some would say that's a bad return, but that's not the point of the story. The point is the investing. That's where the joy is found.

Our greatest fears often revolve around the gifts God has loaned to us, don't they? The more we have, the more we fear. Studies show that the more money we make, the less money proportionally we are likely to give away.

Anne Lamott had this to say about perfectionism:

> I think perfectionism is based on the obsessive belief that if you run carefully enough, hitting each stepping-stone just right, you won't have to die. The truth is you will die anyway and that a lot of people who aren't even looking at their feet are going to do a whole lot better than you, and have a lot more fun while they are doing it.

A fundamental truth about life is that what you have is not your own. *All* of what you have is a gift of grace. The strength you have to get where you're going each day is not your strength; it's God's strength that he gave you. The voice by which you speak is not your voice; it's God's voice that he gave you. The forgiveness you feel is not your forgiveness; it's God's forgiveness that he gave you. The talent you possess—one, two, five, one hundred, two hundred, five hundred talents, whatever you possess—is not your talent; it is God's talent. Whatever resources you have are the gift of grace given you by God.

And for the master, it's all about the joy. And the joy is found in the investing.

I was struck when I read an article about fifty-eight-year-old Philip Lore, a staff sergeant in the New Jersey Army National Guard and a grandfather of six. Decades ago he fought in Vietnam and was awarded the Purple Heart and the Bronze Star. He signed on later to the National Guard, and he's retired from his civilian job now. At age fifty-eight Philip Lore and his unit were deployed to Iraq. At his age, he can appeal his deployment; he's too close to sixty to go. But he doesn't look at it this way. He thinks that he is uniquely gifted. No one else in his unit has seen war. No one has been in a battle. He has the gift of experience, and the great equation says that life's greatest joy is found in the risky investment of our gifts. He wants to go because he wants to help his comrades. One of them said, "What he's done, what he's seen, what he knows, is going to save somebody's life."

Is it true that what gifts you've been given by the master could save somebody's life? I don't suppose you'll ever know until you take your talent from the mattress and with invest it with great risk. That's where the joy is, and joy is what the master is all about.

GOD-SIZED EXPECTATIONS

John 13:1–20

ANTHONY DE MELLO tells the story about the man who took great pride in his lawn. Nothing gave him greater joy than to have the best lawn in the neighborhood. He fertilized it. He limed it. He watered it. He cut it. It was nearly a perfect lawn—except that he had dandelions. Every spring the dandelions would sprout and bare their yellow faces to him as he sat on his front porch. He tried everything to get rid of them: weed killer, digging, the local lawn chemical company. Nothing seemed to work. Finally, when he had exhausted everything he knew to do, he wrote to the Department of Agriculture. He explained all the things he had tried to get rid of these blasted things and begged for advice on what do with these dandelions. A few days later a letter arrived in the mail: "Mr. Smith, thank you for your letter outlining the problems you are having with your dandelions. We understand all the things you've done to try to rid your yard of them. We have only one more thing to suggest. Mr. Smith—we suggest you learn to love them."

In the Gospel of John's description of Jesus's life and ministry, ten of the twenty-one chapters—nearly half—deal with the last week of his life: Palm Sunday to Good Friday to Easter and the appearances after Easter. It's as if John is telling us, "Listen to what Jesus says during this period. Watch what Jesus does. Pay careful attention. Important things happen. I'm focusing here for a reason."

There's certainly a lot to pay attention to. I'd need the rest of this sermon just to list what happens. So in John 13 we watch carefully and see a very interesting thing that Jesus does. In preparation for the Passover—as he gathers with the disciples and with knowledge that Judas has it in his mind to betray him, and realizing moreover that the other disciples are not going to do much better—Jesus takes a basin of water and a towel, and he washes his disciples' feet. He has no business washing the disciples' feet. He is the teacher and the leader. He is the one in the position to have his own feet washed. But Jesus turns it around, and to this group of men who are just about ready to head to Splitsville Jesus says, "Before you go, let me show you how much you're loved. Let me wash your dusty, dirty feet."

Jesus washes the disciples' feet knowing that he also has something to say, maybe the most important thing he has to say: "I have a new commandment. It is the first commandment. It is the most important commandment—that you love one another. As I have loved you, you also should love one another. This will be the thing that reveals your discipleship, if you love one another. You may think you have a lot of important things to do. But the new commandment is to love one another."

The people of God had obviously heard before this commandment to love one another, but they had never heard that it was a commandment above the other ones. It's like the question on the test that's worth ninety-five points. It doesn't matter how well you get the other questions right, if you don't get the 95 percenter correct, forget how right you are on the other ones. It explains the foot washing, doesn't it? Only the type of God who stoops as low as to wash dirty feet can place at the top of the commandment list, "Love one another."

When we take that commandment at face value, those three words—"Love one another"—are huge. Jesus put them at the top of the commandment list because he knows that they cover just about every other law. In the other Gospels, Jesus says, "The two greatest commandments are love the Lord your God with all your heart, soul, strength and mind, and your neighbor as yourself—on these two commandments hang all the law and the prophets."

If you take these commandments at face value, then you have things pretty much figured out . . . but I'm not sure I like the face value! I like helping God to understand my exceptions to the rule. "Lord, when you say, 'Love one another,' you don't mean the guy who double-crossed me. You don't mean the woman who hurt me or the person who slighted me. What your commandment meant to say is, 'Love when it is a pretty good bet that you'll get loved back.'"

But that, of course, is not the word that John uses to report Jesus's commandment of "Love one another." The Greek word is *agape*—a love that expects nothing in return. "Agape one another."

The new commandment is enormous, and it makes all the sense in the world. We would we expect no less from the Creator of the universe. Do you think that if God could leave us with only one, all-encompassing commandment, it would be easily fit into our lives? What do we really think about God?

The story is told of St. Augustine walking along the seashore and noticing a little child sitting at the water's edge. He had dug a hole in the sand, and with every wave that came to the shore, he was trying to gather the water to put into the hole. Augustine watched this for a while, and it dawned on him that we all try to do this. We encounter the life and teaching of God, and we think that somehow—with enough exceptions to the rule—we can make it fit into our lives. But it was never supposed to fit! It was supposed to be God-sized. God is trying to expand us with God-sized expectations.

Learn to love those dandelions. Expand your life so that the unlovable can be loved.

During the civil rights struggle a little town in Mississippi had a boycott of the downtown merchants, organized by black church leaders. It was a peaceful and constructive demonstration, but the police were not on their side and handled them pretty roughly. At the very apex of the struggle, the police chief suffered a heart attack and was in the hospital for several weeks. Even though he was confined to a private room in the hospital, he continued to supervise the police effort, calling deputies to his room every day for reports.

One day one of his men said, "Well, they are planning a rally tonight at the AME church. They say it's going to be a 'prayer' meeting."

"'Prayer meeting,'" the chief snorted. "I'll tell you what. It's a warm night; they'll have the windows open. I want you to go over there and sneak beneath the windows and listen to what they're planning. Give me a report tomorrow."

The next day the deputy returned.

"Did you do as I said?" the chief asked.

"Yes, sir, I did," said the deputy.

"Well, what happened?"

"Well, they sang some hymns."

"Of course, then what happened?"

"Well, they prayed."

"I bet they did. What they pray for?"

"Well, sir, they prayed for you. They prayed for you."

What might we expect from the God of the universe? A commandment that fits snuggly into the compartment of our soul? If we were to ask God boldly to come into our lives, wouldn't we expect that God has some remodeling and expansion plans? Some pushing out of our comfort zone?

Alvin Straight lived in Laurens, Iowa. Alvin was seventy-three years old when he received a call that his brother had had a stroke and was not doing well. Alvin was blind enough to have lost his driver's license, so he had no way to get himself to his brother, who lived in Mount Zion, Wisconsin—240 miles away. Alvin did the only thing he knew to do, which was pull out his 1966 John Deere riding lawnmower and try driving it. Five miles an hour was as fast as it would go, but he went. He pulled behind him a little ten- foot trailer to carry his belongings. Four days into the trip his engine blew, so he had to wait to get someone to fix that. When he got about 90 miles away he ran out of money. He had to wait to the beginning of the month to get his Social Security check forwarded to him. Five miles away from his brother, the mower broke again, so a farmer pushed him into town. But he got there, forty days later.

Love—face-value love, *agape* love, God-sized love—has this way of expanding you.

I've mentioned having my football game interrupted by the broadcast of Anwar Sadat's arrival to Israel. Anwar Sadat—the Arab terrorist, the one who wished Israelis dead, the one who had everything to lose if he offered Israel an olive branch. Indeed he lost his life for his convictions and his actions. Anwar Sadat said,

> When a man's heart is animated by love, he is naturally impelled to accomplish his vocation. Without love, a man may grow very old indeed and yet feel he hasn't lived at all; he would feel he has missed a very important thing—that, however great his achievement, he has really achieved nothing.

Sounds like the apostle Paul when he said,

> If I speak in the tongues of mortals and of angels, but have not love, I am a noisy gong or a clanging cymbal. If I have prophetic power, and understand all mysteries and all knowledge, and if I have all faith so as to remove mountains, but have not love, I am nothing. If I give away my body so that I may boast, but have not love, I gain nothing.

As he gets up off the floor from washing dirty feet, this One who was there at the beginning of the universe, this One who was there when the Big Bang banged and set the universe into an ever-expanding expansion, why would Jesus not want to expand us? To leave us the all-expanding command, the God-sized expectation for our lives, the very gift that animates us and makes us larger than ourselves?

But what about my enemy, Jesus? What about the person I can't stand to be around? What about the double-crosser? What about the person who hurt me so much?

"I suggest," Jesus says, "no, actually I command that you learn to love them."

Illio costalis cerviq!
↓ musck
Thoacas

Longissimus
Thoracis
cervializ musck

Made in the USA
San Bernardino, CA
01 December 2015